rororo

rororo sprachen
Herausgegeben von Ludwig Moos

rororo

Ob zwischen Kollegen, innerhalb von Hierarchien oder im Umgang mit Kunden – die Kunst der Kommunikation ist der Schlüssel für den geschäftlichen Erfolg. Übt man sie in der Weltsprache des Business, kommt das Beachten interkultureller Unterschiede noch hinzu. *How to Communicate Effectively* hilft Ihnen mit seiner einprägsamen Story, meist in Dialogen, und einem Programm ausgefeilter Übungen, die sprachlichen und psychologischen Fertigkeiten zu schulen, damit Sie andere besser verstehen und selbst richtig verstanden werden.

Dr. René Bosewitz ist Native Speaker und bereitet in einer deutschen Zweigstelle der London Chamber of Commerce Firmenangehörige auf einschlägige sprachliche Prüfungen vor. Er trainiert zudem seit vielen Jahren Manager aus Banken und Industrie in Business English. Bei rororo sprachen hat er *Better Your English* (60802) und *Perfect Your English* (61147), zusammen mit Robert Kleinschroth *Joke Your Way Through English Grammar* (8527) und *Joke by Joke to Conversation* (8795) veröffentlicht.

Robert Kleinschroth unterrichtet Englisch am Gymnasium und an der Universität Heidelberg. Er hat zwanzig Jahre Praxis in der Erwachsenenbildung und leitete fünfzehn Jahre lang die Sprachabteilung eines Großunternehmens. Robert Kleinschroth hat zusammen mit Dieter Maupai *La Grammaire en s'amusant* (8714) verfasst und außerdem *La Conversation en s'amusant* (8873) sowie *Sprachen lernen* (9140) geschrieben.

In der Reihe Business English sind von beiden Autoren außerdem erschienen:
Manage in English (60137), *Better than the Boss* (60138), *How to Phone Effectively* (60139), *Drop Them a Line* (60261, mit Bryan Hemming), *Get Through at Meetings* (60262), *Check Your Language Level* (60268), *Business English from A to Z* (60269, mit Bryan Hemming), *The Way Things Work* (60369), *Small Talk for Big Business* (60439), *Sell like Hell* (60722), *Master Your Business Phrases* (60725), *Get to Grips with Company English* (60845), *Spice up Your Speeches* (60804), *Better Your Business English* (60846) und *Making Money on the Web* (60368).

RENÉ BOSEWITZ/ROBERT KLEINSCHROTH

HOW TO COMMUNICATE EFFECTIVELY

VERSTEHEN UND VERSTANDEN WERDEN IM BUSINESS

ROWOHLT TASCHENBUCH VERLAG

Wir danken Frau Gitta Most für ihre Hilfe bei der Korrektur der Fahnen und Frau Ellen Hahn für die Unterstützung bei der Erstellung des Manuskripts.

Originalausgabe
Veröffentlicht im Rowohlt Taschenbuch Verlag GmbH,
Reinbek bei Hamburg, Oktober 2001

Umschlaggestaltung Barbara Hanke
(Illustration Cathrin Günther)
Layout Anne Drude
Satz OCRA und Stone, PostScript Linotype Library,
QuarkXPress 4.0
Druck und Bindung Clausen & Bosse, Leck
Printed in Germany
ISBN 3 499 61146 5

Sie wollen Karriere und gute Geschäfte machen? Dann müssen Sie ein guter Kommunikator werden. Sie müssen sich und Ihr Produkt so präsentieren, dass Sie angenommen werden.

Mit *How to Communicate Effectively* verbessern Sie Ihre *communication skills* und Ihr Englisch. Kommunikation in der Fremdsprache ist gerade für uns Deutsche wichtig, weil Deutschland über die Fremdsprache exportiert. Wir haben siebzehn typische Situationen herausgegriffen und mit einer lockeren *story line* verbunden. Es sind Situationen, in die man im Geschäftsleben immer wieder kommt: Interview, Besprechung, Präsentation, Rede, Smalltalk, Coaching, Telefonieren, Schreiben, Beschweren und Werbung, um nur einige zu nennen.

Am Anfang eines jeden Kapitels steht ein Dialog zum Thema, über den Sie in unserer *Analyst's Corner* nachdenken sollen. Natürlich geht es auch um Business English und die Redemittel, die für die Situation nützlich sind und die Sie in kurzen Übungen vertiefen sollen. Die Lösungen dazu finden Sie im Anhang. Nützliches *know-how* zu jeder Situation und ausgewählte Redemittel finden Sie in der *Communicator's Corner* beziehungsweise der *Psychologist's Corner.*

Werden Sie ein guter Kommunikator, auch in der Fremdsprache, denn Kommunikation war noch nie so wichtig wie heute. Viele meinen sogar, gute Kommunikation sei entscheidender für den Erfolg einer Firma als die Qualität ihrer Produkte. Ohne Kommunikation nach innen und außen keine Geschäfte, keine Karriere. *Read on!*
Viel Spaß und Erfolg!

Busoom Ltd depends on communication skills

At no other time in the history of big business and giant corporations, has good communication been more important. Most problems can be traced back to failures in communication. On the other hand, the person with polished oral and written communication skills advances more rapidly. Ask any Human Resources manager and he will tell you that their primary reason for rejecting applicants is poor communication skill. Many actors on the stage of life are not even aware that this skill or the lack of it decides whether they will achieve their aims and desires or not. They cannot understand why they are misunderstood or disliked. And in terms of the business world this can mean wrong decisions or no decision at all.

The bosses at Busoom Ltd know that the success of an organization depends on the communication skills of its employees at all levels. You might have heard about that company – if not let's fill you in.
They sell electronic, automatic door systems (you know, those doors that spin around by themselves at stores like Oldie, Horden, Buy-Yard and others. Hospitals have them, too). The company is a subsidiary of a Swedish parent company. They all bear the same name and are enjoying success and growth, but problems arise from this, too. And most of these troubles originate in communication, or rather the lack of it.
That's what this book is about. In the next two hundred or so golden pages we will meet many situations based on communication problems and we will read about possible solutions.

We'll get to know the following characters who run the company.

- John Hardman, CEO
- Herbert Seaweed, Director of Personnel and Administration (his friends call him Weedy)
- Dr Geisel, Technology Director + After Sales
- David Ramsch, Director of Production
- No Name, Operations Manager
- Mrs Velvet, Personal Assistant to the CEO, and other slaves

WORD AID

WORD AID

achieve one's aims	*seine Ziele erreichen*
applicant	*Bewerber*
avoid	*vermeiden*
bear the same name	*den gleichen Namen tragen*
counsellor	*Berater*
emphasis	*Betonung, Schwerpunkt*
enjoy one's success	*seinen Erfolg genießen*
depend on	*abhängen von*
fill someone in on something	*jemanden über etwas aufklären / unterrichten*
growth	*Wachstum*
Human Resources manager	*Personalchef*
lack	*Mangel*
oral	*mündlich*
originate in	*herrühren von*
parent company	*Muttergesellschaft*
primary reasons	*hauptsächliche Gründe*
reject	*ablehnen*
self-confidence	*Selbstvertrauen*
skill	*Fertigkeit*
slave	*Sklave*
spin around	*sich drehen (um die eigene Achse)*
stress	*betonen*
subsidiary	*Tochtergesellschaft*
trace failures back to	*Fehler zurückverfolgen bis*

Think positive

To gain self-confidence, you must avoid using negative words such as "can't" and "not," the counsellor advised the young woman, "Do you think you could do that?"
"Well, I can't see why not."

PRESENTING YOURSELF

YOU DON'T GET A SECOND CHANCE TO MAKE A GOOD IMPRESSION

In the background to *How to Communicate Effectively* you encountered our corporate hero, Busoom GmbH. Busoom's Personnel Director, Mr Seaweed (some people call him Weedy) is interviewing a potential candidate for the position of technical manager. Here we are not interested in Seaweed's interviewing techniques. Those will be praised in a later chapter. What concerns us here is how the candidate presents himself. What are the tricks in this area of communication?

We focus on

- how to make the right impression
- the vocabulary of losers and winners
- the psychology of the first five minutes
- and a few jokes about applying for a job

You don't get a second chance to make a good impression

Let's listen in on the conversation between Mr Lost (**L**) and Mr Seaweed (**S**).

S: Well, that was very interesting hearing about your adventures as a student. I've got the impression that you're still rather, how can I put it, laid-back. I mean in your attitude to working life.[1]

L: You could put it like that. After all, it's not the outer appearance that's important. It's what you know. It's results that count.
(Perhaps we should mention here that Lost was dressed in blue jeans, had a pony tail in his hair and an earring in his well-polished ears. Not that we will make any value judgement on any of these things. Not at all!)

S: Yes, I'm sure you're right, but are you sure that an eight or ten-hour day in the research department would be the right thing for you? I mean how did you achieve your objectives in your present company?

L: In the company I'm with now? Well, things just took care of themselves. I was given a task and I reached my targets on time. No problem![2]

S: I see. To come to another point. I'd be very interested to hear how you see the next five years of your professional life. What do you want personally?

L: I'm enjoying my work at present, but I don't really have any fixed plans for the next years. I'd like to do my job well. Let's let the rest take care of itself.[3] I mean it's important to have any job at all nowadays with twenty million unemployed in Europe.

S: Quite! That's one way of looking at it. Tell me, in your present company have you had any specially difficult tasks to do? Any challenging situations?

L: Yes, there were quite a few things, but I got over them easily enough. That's why they employed me at the end of the day, isn't it?[4]

S: I'm sure it was. Well, I guess I've got a pretty good idea about your background. By the way, I'm sure there must be some questions from your side. Fire away!

1 The numbers in the text refer to the explanations in the Analyst's Corner.

L: No, Mr Seaweed, actually you've described everything very completely. Thank you.[5]

S: Fine. Well, in that case we'll be in touch with you in the next few weeks. Thank you for coming.

The Analyst's Corner

Although this case was a job interview, the same "rules" are valid for when you meet anybody at work for the first time. Let's look at poor old Lost's mistakes.

1. Seaweed has clearly noticed Lost's dress and his whole attitude. Lost thinks it's important what you do and not what you look like. Although there is truth in this, it is also important to follow some rules, and not to be a square peg in a round hole. This might upset the team. And the other point is that a candidate should show interest and determination; he should make a special effort. And that includes appearance.

2. When asked about your present work you should describe it, explain your part and contribution. Lost's "Well, things just took care of themselves" was a very pale answer.

3. Seaweed asks about Mr Lost's plans for the future. Lost, taking it very easy, says he has none. This creates the bad impression that a candidate has not given any thought to this question.

4. Seaweed asks for some impressions on how Lost tackles issues at his present company. Lost, once more, does not present his tactics or solutions: "I got over them easily enough. That's why they employed me." Bad answer! No communication!

5. A candidate should always have some of his own questions. It shows interest, real ambition to land the job. Nothing came from Lost's side. Overall he has created a weak impression – no job!

WORKING with the language

TASK 1: Business phrases to remember

Please fill in the gaps.

we'll get back to you	we'll be in ________ ____ you
the results are important	it's results that ________
let's try and solve the problem	let's ________ the problem
he didn't get the job	he didn't ________ the job
a subsidiary belongs to it	a subsidiary belongs to a ________ ________

TASK 2: First words

Please complete these polite noises.

Good morning. ________ ____ you?	________, thank you.
Nice to ________ you.	It's ________ to ______ you.
________ to meet you.	The ________ is mine.

Creating a winner's image

One reason why poor Mr Lost didn't land the job was his vocabulary. He used pale and passive phrases like

> I *was given* a task ...
> There *were quite a few* things ...
> I got over them *easily enough* ...

- Show that you're actively achieving things in your work.
- Start sentences with dynamic verbs.
- Use positive adverbs to convey how your tasks were performed.

Losers	Winners
worked on customer service	*improved* service to customers
dealt with suppliers	*negotiated better terms* with suppliers
was involved in business development	*streamlined processes and procedures*
did clerical work	*established / improved administrative systems*

Here are the winners to create a dynamic image

Verbs: Don't use *do, make* and *work* – instead use

increase	improve	streamline
identify	reduce	establish
develop	initiate	negotiate
produce	launch	organise
design	motivate	co-ordinate
satisfy	save	create
solve	suggest	mount

Nouns: Don't use *job* and *thing* – use

goals	achievements	responsibility
objectives	benefit	result
aims	profit	advantage
target	solution	campaign
performance	satisfaction	fulfilment

Use dynamic adverbs and adjectives like

successful(ly)	competitive	booming
efficient(ly)	profitable	reliable
effective(ly)	satisfactory	trendy
considerable(-bly)	beneficial	modern

TASK 3: Streamlining Lost's language

Now use the winners from our tables to replace the losers.
We've helped you with the first letters.

There *were quite a few* things to do in our department ...	I *i*_______________ problems in our department ...
... and I *got over* the problems *easily enough.*	... and I *s*_______________ solutions that *s*_______________ our problems once and for all.
I *handled* the *advertising* for ...	I *m*_____________ a successful advertising *c*___________ for ...
I *helped to market* our new X15.	I *l*_____________ our new X 15 and ___________ its profitability.
I *was involved* in personnel training.	I *s*__________ trained staff.
I *was given* a *task* ...	I *a*_____________ my targets to the fullest *s*_______________ of my superiors.

TASK 4: Increase your word power

1. Do you remember the four expressions for the German *Ziel*?
2. On the following page we use three synonyms for *mean*. Maybe you know already one.
3. And there are also three words for *nachmachen / anpassen*. Find them.

The Psychologist's Corner

How to present yourself

No second chance to make a good impression

The first minutes are the most important in a meeting. The conversation which follows will be filtered through the favourable impression you make during the first five minutes.

Have a positive mental attitude

because we are drawn to people who are enthusiastic, passionate, optimistic and happy.

Smile

and you accomplish four powerful things:

1. It means **happiness** – we prefer happy people to gloomy ones.
2. It signals **confidence** and makes us feel comfortable – people who are nervous don't smile.
3. It conveys **enthusiasm** – and enthusiasm is contagious.
4. It shows **acceptance**. Smiling is a sign that we accept the other person and the situation.

Be in sync

and build a psychological bridge to your partners. Be one of them. Be dressed like them. Match their clothes and colours, mirror their posture, movements and speech. If your partner speaks in a relaxed, slow tone, do the same; if he puts his hand in his pocket then imitate him. We like persons who are like us (see also Module 2).

Having things in common

Like attracts like. Before you first meet important persons try to find out about their hobbies, their families, the cars they drive, the books they read etc. A call to their secretaries might help you. We like those people who are like us, who have similar interests. So mention what you both enjoy, talk about what you have in common.

Appear young

Youthfulness is a factor of physical attractiveness. The good news is that you needn't be young to appear youthful. **Flexibility** will make you appear youthful. Yoga will produce a dramatic difference in your posture, your body language and the way you walk and talk (see above: dynamic vocabulary).

The IMPACT-Formula

Six golden rules on how to make a good impression

The first meeting is the most important moment in a relationship.
You never get a second chance to make a good impression.

I ntegrity: be honest and truthful with business partners.
M anners: never be selfish, rude or undisciplined.
P ersonality: communicate your own values and opinions.
A ppearance: wear suitable clothes, stand and sit with a good posture.
C onsideration: see yourself from the other person's standpoint.
T act: think before you speak; avoid religion, sex and politics.

Communicating in interviews

Be a good interviewee

- Collect information about the company.
  Will they need you?
  Will you find the right working conditions?
  Can they offer you perspectives?
- Prepare information about yourself.
  What are your reasons for applying to this company?
  What do you expect?
  What have you achieved in your present job? Give concrete examples of your work performance.
  Have you ever had to make an important decision?
- Support your answers with examples.
- Have questions ready to ask about the company and your future job.

TASK 5: Communication quiz

Find out more about yourself and the secrets of communication. Choose the five communication needs / styles which you think are the most important ones for you.

Das Gefühl ...

1. man akzeptiert mich	to feel accepted
2. man respektiert mich	to feel respected
3. man bewundert mich	to feel admired
4. man versteht mich	to feel understood
5. man gibt mir Sicherheit	to feel reassured
6. man schätzt mich	to feel appreciated
7. man mag mich	to feel cared about
8. man stimmt mir zu	to feel approved of
9. man erhält Bestätigung	to feel validated
10. man vertraut mir	to feel trusted

Now go to the Key, page 214, and find out who you are and why this test is important for your communication skills.

Time for a smile

"So you love my daughter and you want to marry her," said the boss to the young man. "Well, write out your qualifications, name and address and any other details you think appropriate and leave it with my secretary. If no other suitable applicants turn up, we will ask you to come for a further interview."

WORD AID

achieve	*leisten, vollbringen*
achievement	*Leistung*
administrative systems	*Verwaltungssysteme, -apparate*
After Sales	*Kundendienst*
ambition	*Ehrgeiz*
appearance	*Erscheinung*
apply for a job	*sich für einen Posten bewerben*
apply to	*sich bewerben bei*
appropriate	*passend, angemessen*
attractiveness	*Attraktivität*
beneficial	*vorteilhaft*
benefit	*Vorteil*
body language	*Körpersprache*
bottom line	*hier: Fazit, Ergebnis*
challenging situations	*Situationen, die eine Herausforderung sind*
clerical work	*Büroarbeit*
competitive	*wettbewerbsfähig*
concern someone	*jemanden betreffen*
confidence	*Zuversicht, Vertrauen*
considerable	*beträchtlich*
contagious	*ansteckend*
corporate hero	*Firmenheld*
count	*zählen*
count; it's results that ~	*nur Ergebnisse zählen*
determination	*Entschlossenheit*
display passion	*Leidenschaft zeigen*
impact	*Eindruck, Wirkung*
involved in	*beteiligt an*
judgement	*Urteil*
laid-back	*ganz sorglos, entspannt*
land a job	*eine Stelle bekommen*
listen in on someone	*jemandem bei etwas zuhören*

mount a campaign	*eine Kampagne starten*
parent company	*Muttergesellschaft*
peg	*Pflock*
praise	*loben*
press aid	*Assistent des Pressesprechers*
procedure	*Vorgehen, Verfahren*
processes	*Geschäftsabläufe*
research department	*Forschungsabteilung*
responsibility	*Verantwortung*
solution	*Lösung*
satisfy	*befriedigen*
square	*viereckig*
streamline	*verschlanken, beschleunigen*
submit an application	*eine Bewerbung einreichen*
subsidiary	*Tochtergesellschaft*
succeed in	*Erfolg haben bei*
suitable	*geeignet, passend*
supplier	*Lieferant*
support	*(unter)stützen*
sync; be in sync	*auf der gleichen Wellenlänge sein*
tackle issues	*Dinge, Probleme in Angriff nehmen*
target; reach targets	*Ziele erreichen*
task	*Aufgabe*
tasks; do ~	*Aufgaben erfüllen*
touch; be in ~ with	*in Verbindung stehen*
value judgement	*Werturteil*

Time for a smile

Ron: "I've heard you applied for that job at the film studio. How was the interview?"

Tom: "Difficult. I had to ride a horse for three hours."

Ron: "And did you get the job?"

Tom: "No, but the horse did."

2 Module

THE ART OF LISTENING

TALKING AT CROSS-PURPOSES

In any form of discussion whether it is a negotiation, a conference, meeting, or the often misquoted small talk, the key to success and to a positive result is to listen and be seen to be listening. In the following we have a typical top management meeting at Busoom. Watch for the misunderstandings, notice when a manager does not really listen.

We focus on

- the nature of active listening and mirroring
- the power of listening
- polite noises while listening
- and famous flops in communication

Talking at cross-purposes

Present are Hardman, CEO (**H**), Seaweed (**S**), Dr Geisel (**G**). They are discussing the installation of an automatic swing door in the company at Deadbug.

H: ... and so I'd like to give you an overview of three items that we have dealt with since our last meeting. Please look at the flipchart.
(He turns the pages which are all covered in scribble. There is no space to write. For that matter there are no marker pens, either.)
For God's sake! Where's a clean flipchart?
(Hardman whips his mobile out of a leather pouch on his belt.) Mrs Velvet, the flipchart is used up. Please bring another one immediately. What? Where? Oh, over there in the corner. Well, I didn't know that. This is no operational excellence, as the Americans say. Thank you.

S: I don't like to mention it, Mr Hardman, but Mrs Velvet explained where everything was to you yesterday at our Operations Meeting. Perhaps you didn't hear her.[1]

H: Possibly. It was very loud at the meeting. Everybody was shouting. Now, first of all to the revolving door near the reception desk. I've been waiting for weeks for a solution.

G: Well, a lot happened this week. The doors arrived from Sweden. I inspected everything personally. I found them to be okay. I supervised the installation myself and they were in operation last Wednesday. Production were very satisfied.

H: Satisfied!? How could they be content? The work hadn't even begun. I can't see where you're coming from[2]. Where's the operational excellence? Without information I can't make decisions. I walked through the reception area half an hour ago and there was no installation.[3]

G: That can't be. I signed the installation off myself. I ...[2]
(Seaweed interrupts.)

S: Gentlemen, I think we're talking at cross-purposes. Mr Hardman, which revolving door are you talking about[3]?

---

1 The numbers in the text refer to the questions in the Analyst's Corner and to the answers in the Key.

G: *(grunting)* Oh, now I see.

S: And you, Dottore, which door?

G: I see the problem now. The door from the main building to production.

H: Oh my God! What a waste of the company's valuable time.

G: The revolver at reception will be installed by next morning. It's all fixed.

H: Well, thank you for that. Next, I see problems with our whole telephone system. That's my second point today. It's like a black cloud on the Busoom horizon. Mr Seaweed. Status please!

S: It's all been complicated. There were several suppliers involved and there were different suggestions.

H: Weedy, I asked you for status, not for a presentation about the complications.

S: Okay, to the point then. I've contacted Dutch Telecrap. I asked them to check out our needs and suggest an optimal system.

H: Dutch Telecrap? They are a bunch of robbers. And I'm as far from satisfied as I can be. I watch them doing nothing. I read their blurbs. It's just blinding people.[4] Well, did they propose a solution for our phones and software?

S: Actually, there were some problems.

H: I bet there were. That's just what I expected. They don't understand service in the year 2001. I ... *(Seaweed interrupts)*

S: I know we've had some problems with Telecrap, but should I understand that you insist that we find another supplier?[5]

G: To be fair, from a technical point of view they have a lot of pluspoints.

H: Pluspoints? Okay, Dottore, come to the chart. Let's list the points up ...

The Analyst's Corner

TASK 1: Sit back and think

The numbers in our dialogue refer to these questions:

1. How could Hardman have improved the communication leading up to "everyone was shouting"?
2. How did the communication problem occur in this situation?
3. From "satisfied to[3]," Hardman's behaviour is unprofessional – why?
4. What type of communicative language is Hardman using here? How might a professional communicator have reacted?
5. What tactic is Seaweed using here?

WORKING with the language

TASK 2: Enlarge your business English

einen Überblick über die Themen geben	give an __________ of the __________
sich mit einem Problem / Kunden befassen	______ ____ a problem / a customer
auf eine Lösung warten	wait ____ a __________
aneinander vorbeireden	be talking ___ ______-purposes
Verschwendung wertvoller Zeit	__________ of __________ time
nach dem Stand der Dinge fragen	ask ____ a ______ report
jemandes Bedürfnisse / Bedarf überprüfen	check someone's __________
in Betrieb sein	be in ______________

TASK 3: Bits and pieces

1. Translate the German in brackets:
   We have dealt with three items (*seit*) our last meeting.
   I've been waiting (*seit*) weeks for a solution.

2. Remember the two words for *zufrieden*?
   How could they be (*zufrieden*)?
   Production were very (*zufrieden*).

3. Use an infinitive with *to*:
   I find that the doors are okay.
   There is no space where one can *write*.

The Psychologist's Corner

Active listening and mirroring

Are you an active listener? Do you know when to speak and when to listen? Here's some advice for you! Take it, become an active listener and you will

- be liked by those you listen to (see page 28),
- be trusted and inspire confidence,
- win time during meetings to understand a problem more fully,
- win time to study the personality of your opposite number.

Three types

Studying their personality is important. Listen to their language and find out which type of person you have to do with. Are they the

- auditive,
- visual or
- emotional type?

You can use your knowledge to harmonize a conversation, to take the tension out of a situation. Speak their language and you will create a rapport with them and they will understand you better. You will win their trust. And if they trust you, you will find it easier to do business with them. We will show you how to identify these types in later chapters.

Speak their language

Now this is what you should do after listening and analysing. Be their mirror, match their language.

- Use the vocabulary of the visual person, and he or she will see eye to eye with you.
- Adopt the vocabulary of the auditive type and he will listen to you for a longer time than he had originally planned.
- Tune in to the emotional caller and he will feel at home with you.

There is more you can do

- Adapt your tempo of speaking to the caller's speed. He will understand you better.
- Don't speak louder than the person you are talking to.
- Speak the other person's dialect – but only if it's yours.
- Avoid dialect if the caller speaks Hochdeutsch or standard English.
- Use body language. If a person strongly disagrees with you, he will be sitting defensively. Carefully mirror this posture and slowly change it into a more open one. This will encourage him to be less defensive.

How to keep the ball rolling

Listening actively means encouraging a person to continue talking. Encouraging means showing interest and providing feedback to the speaker. Thus you can influence what might or might not be said. How is this done?

By words, of course, and by body language. Here are five categories of very simple speech functions that encourage discussion partners to go on talking and to help you to learn more about them.

1. Moderate **praise**: Not bad at all!
2. Showing **interest**: Oh! How interesting!
3. Showing **astonishment**: Well, well, well! Fancy that!
4. **Agreeing**: Quite true. Quite right.
5. Slight and moderate **disagreeing**: Is that so? Really?

6. Showing **sympathy**: It's a great loss to all of us.

These speech functions might avoid embarrassing silences during a conversation. They give you and your partner time to think and to formulate the message accurately. And what is more important – you win time to analyse the other party. Do you understand these signals? Well here's a test for you.

TASK 4: Communication practice

Five ways to encourage a person to open his or her heart to you:

1. Moderate praise
2. Showing interest
3. Slight astonishment
4. Agreeing, accepting
5. Disagreeing moderately
6. Showing sympathy

Are you able to identify and use them in a conversation?
Then write the right number in the boxes.

I can imagine how you must feel.	
Would you believe it?	
Tell me more.	
I wonder.	
Definitely!	
Incredible!	
Well done!	
How extraordinary!	
You don't say so!	
I can't blame you.	
Really?	
Good for you!	
Who knows?	
Of course!	
I know what it's like.	

TASK 5: Active listener's treasure chest

A. Active listeners fill the pauses with comments of polite astonishment.

Das ist erstaunlich.	It's ____________ .
Unglaublich!	In__________! Un__________!
Das ist einmalig / unerhört!	That ________ everything!

B. These polite noises signal that you are interested in a story.

Erzählen Sie mir mehr davon.	Please, ________ me ________
Das ist höchst interessant.	That's _______ interesting.
Tolle Geschichte!	___________ a story!

C. Being accepted and respected is a basic human need. But be honest!

Ich sehe das auch so.	I think _____ , ___.
Ich verstehe, was Sie meinen.	I ________ your point.
Ich bin ganz Ihrer Meinung.	I absolutely _______ with you.
Sie treffen den Nagel auf den Kopf.	You've ____ the nail on the _____.

D. Doubt can be stimulating – but be careful!

Sind Sie sicher?	Are you _________?
Ist das wirklich Ihr Ernst?	Do you really _______that?
Was Sie nicht sagen!	You don't _________!
Kaum zu glauben!	Can you _________it?

Flops in communication

I've made good judgements in the past, I've made good judgements in the future.
It's time for the human race to enter the solar system.
I am not part of the problem. I am a Democrat.
Al Gore, Ex-Vice-president

The Communicator's Corner

The power of listening

Listening is the opposite of interrupting. This is an excerpt from Dale Carnegie, *How to win friends and influence people*. It is a good illustration of how you can make everybody like you just by listening to them.

I was recently invited to a bridge party. Personally, I don't play bridge and there was a blonde there who didn't play bridge, either. She had discovered that I had travelled a great deal. So she said: "Oh, Mr Carnegie, I do want you to tell me about all the wonderful places you have visited and the sights you have seen." As we sat down on the sofa, she remarked that she and her husband had recently returned from a trip to Africa. "Africa!" I exclaimed. "How interesting! I always wanted to see Africa, but I never got there except for a twenty-four-hour stay once in Algiers. Tell me, did you visit the big-game country? Yes? How fortunate! I envy you! Do tell me about Africa."
That was good for forty-five minutes. She never again asked me where I had been or what I had seen. She didn't want to hear me talk about my travels. All she wanted was an interested listener, so she could expand her ego and tell about where she had been.
Was she unusual? No. Many people are like that. For example, I recently met a distinguished botanist at a dinner party given by J. W. Greenberg, the New York book publisher. I had never talked to a botanist before, and I found him fascinating. I literally sat on the edge of my chair and listened while he spoke of hashish and Luther Burbank and indoor gardens and told me astonishing facts about the humble potato ...
Midnight came. I said good night to everyone and departed. The botanist then turned to our host and paid me several flattering compliments. I was "most stimulating." I was this and I was that; and he ended up by saying I was a "most interesting conversationalist."

An interesting conversationalist? I? Why, I had said hardly anything at all. I couldn't have said anything if I had wanted to without changing the subject, for I don't know any more about botany than I know about the anatomy of a penguin. But I had done this: I had listened intently. I had listened because I was interested.

Flops in communication

If we don't succeed, we run the risk of failure.
The future will be better tomorrow.
We're going to have the best-educated American people in the world.
Al Gore, Ex-Vice-president

WORD AID

annoyed	*verärgert*
apply for a job	*sich für einen Posten bewerben*
appropriate	*passend, angemessen*
astonishment	*Erstaunen*
avoid	*vermeiden*
big-game	*Großwild*
blurb	*Stuss, Schwachsinn*
botany	*Botanik*
bunch of robbers	*eine Räuberbande*
chart	*Grafik, Karte*
confidence	*Zuversicht, Vertrauen*
confuse the issue	*das Problem verwechseln*
deal with something	*etwas behandeln*
decision	*Entscheidung*
defensive(ly)	*abweisend*
depart	*aufbrechen*
disagree	*anderer Meinung sein*
distinguished; ~ botanist	*berühmter Botaniker*
distortion	*Entstellung, Verzerrung*
embarrassing silence	*peinliches Schweigen*
exaggeration	*Übertreibung*
expand	*ausweiten, ausbreiten*
flattering compliments	*schmeichelhafte Komplimente*
humble	*schlicht, demütig*
incredible	*unglaublich*
inspire confidence	*Zuversicht, Vertrauen einflößen*
intent	*Absicht*
judgement	*Urteil*
listen intently	*gespannt, aufmerksam zuhören*
literally	*buchstäblich*
loss	*Verlust*
match someone's language	*sich jemandes Sprache anpassen*
most stimulating	*sehr anregend*
need	*Bedürfnis*

operational excellence	*etwa: Effizienz und Qualität auf allen Ebenen*
opposite	*Gegenteil*
opposite number	*Gegenüber, Gesprächspartner*
overhear	*belauschen, mithören*
pay compliments	*Komplimente machen*
pouch	*Tasche, Etui*
praise	*Lob*
press aid	*Assistent des Pressesprechers*
propose a solution	*eine Lösung vorschlagen*
provide feedback	*Rückmeldung geben*
rapport	*Verständnis*
recently	*kürzlich, vor kurzem*
remark	*bemerken*
revolver	*hier: Drehtür*
revolving door	*Drehtür*
scribble	*kritzeln, Kritzelei*
see eye to eye with someone	*sich mit jemandem gut verstehen*
sign off the repair	*eine Reparatur abzeichnen*
sit on the edge of one's chair	*gespannt sein*
Status, please!	*Wie ist der Stand der Dinge?*
stay	*Aufenthalt; bleiben*
submit an application	*eine Bewerbung einreichen*
succeed	*Erfolg haben*
suggestion	*Vorschlag, Anregung*
suitable	*geeignet, passend*
supervise	*überwachen*
supplier	*Lieferant, Zulieferer*
sympathy	*Mitgefühl*
talk at cross-purposes	*aneinander vorbeireden*
tension	*Spannung*
point; to the ~ then	*zur Sache also*
tune in to someone	*sich einfühlen, anpassen*
used up; the flipchart is ~ ~	*das Flipchart ist voll*
whip something out	*etwas blitzschnell hervorholen*

3 Module

GETTING YOUR MESSAGE ACROSS

SMOKE ALARM

As in any other company perhaps the most stressful situations are those linked to people: lack of interpersonal skills, pride, jealousy. All these things play a role. And so it is at Busoom too. The background is that there've been a lot of problems among members of the staff regarding smoking and drinking. What, you might ask, does that mean? If a fellow wants a cigarette or a drink (on special occasions such as birthdays), then why not? So they had the idea to let the smokers go outside the building for a quick fag. "Nothing wrong with that," you say to yourself. Listen in on the following conversation.

We focus on

- written and spoken communication
- how to get your message across
- more about body language

Smoke alarm

Tom (T) and Jim (J), two workers in the production

J: I'll see you a bit later. I'm just off for a minute.
T: Hey, where are you going? You can't just leave your workplace.
J: Yes, I can. I've got a ten-minute smoking break.
T: Hey, just wait a minute. Is that in addition to your tea break in the afternoon?
J: 'Course it is. What do you think?
T: Well, I'm not taking that on board. I want my extra ten minutes as well. That's an hour a week. Just for your bad habits. *(fade out)*

So you see, you've got to be careful. Now, it's the turn of the management. In this case it's Seaweed's (**S**) chance again as he's the director of personnel. He's talking to Dump (**D**), the works council, who has to represent the interests of the workers. Seaweed and Anne, as secretary (**A**).

S: So it's our feeling that we should introduce some special rules. *(He turns squarely to Dump and looks him directly in the eye.)*[1]
D: Well, any rules have got to be fair and not just top down. Now, what's the problem with the smoking?
S: We have to think of the well-being of the majority of our colleagues who are non-smokers. They don't want smoking in their offices.
D: Well, who said that? You can't forbid someone to smoke.
S: It's not a question of forbidding. I want to emphasize, we are responsible for the health of our staff. That must be important for you too.[2]
D: But I don't want people losing their rights.
S: Okay, I'll come to the point.[3] Eighty-five percent want smoking banned from the offices. That means in every office there is a majority that wants no smoking. Therefore there should be no smoking in the offices. The smokers can go outside at lunch or in their break.
D: Hey now! Slowly. We have some rules too, in case you've forgotten. *(Seaweed takes out a pen and a notepad.)*[4]

1 The numbers in the text refer to the questions in the Analyst's Corner and to the answers in the Key.

S: Of course, you're right. I'll just note down your ideas and we'll find a way.

D: The first thing is that you can't simply send somebody out to smoke. The law says you have to provide a room for him to smoke in. And in the end you'll have to allow him the time not as his coffee break but as extra time.

S: If we allow extra time for smoking the non-smokers will feel that they are being swindled. *(He leans forward over the desk and looks intensively at Dump.)* Listen, we have to find a way to work together. We need a result for everybody, don't we? *(There's a knock at the door. Seaweed's secretary comes in.)*[5]

A: There's a phone call for you from Breton GmbH in Hamburg. Should I tell them you'll phone back?

S: Yes please, and I want no further interruptions. Now, where were we?

D: We wanted to reach a common goal. Okay. I realize you've made a survey to see who wants smoking and who doesn't. And we've got to support the majority. I see that. My idea is that we declare certain areas of the company non-smoking and others as smoking.

S: Right. Now, that's a good start. Let's keep all as simple as possible. *(fade out)*

The following day the employees had the following memo in their pigeon holes / mail boxes:

> May 10,2001
> **Memo**: To members of the First Line Management
> **Subject**: Smoking Policy at Busoom.
>
> Since the majority of staff would prefer smoking to be banned from the offices completely, whereas a minority need to smoke we, the Board of Busoom Ltd, have come to the following agreement with the Works Council of Busoom. This provides for a ban on smoking in the offices, but allows certain extra rooms for smokers. The time taken up by smoking must be compensated for by extra time at the workplace.
>
> Hardman, CEO

The Analyst's Corner

TASK 1: Sit back and think

1. How does Seaweed show that he wants to be fair and open to Dump?
2. How does Seaweed emphasize his point about health being important?
3. "Okay, I'll come to the point." What is the effect of the statement and the following text?
4. What's all this about a notepad? Why does Seaweed do this?
5. What's the effect of this interruption?

WORKING with the language

TASK 2: Business phrases to remember

eine zehnminütige Zigarettenpause	a ten-minute ________
etwas akzeptieren, übernehmen	take something on ________
mit dem Betriebsrat sprechen	talk to the ________ ________
die Interessen der Arbeiter vertreten	________ the interests of the workers
besondere Regeln einführen	________ special ________
für das Personal verantwortlich sein	be ________ for the ________
zur Sache kommen	come to the ________
Ich wünsche keine weiteren Unterbrechungen.	I want no ________ ________.
alles so einfach wie möglich halten	________ everything ___ simple ___ possible
die Mehrheit unterstützen	________ the majority

The Communicator's Corner

TASK 3: Rules about communication

Here you learn more about communication. And to practise your English at the same time translate the German in brackets. Here's help for you:

purpose	check	strike
subject	maintain	simple
receive	message	targeted

How to get your message across

1. Communication has two main aspects: to (*aufrechterhalten*) personal relationships and to get your (*Botschaft*) across.
2. In order to get it across you should ask yourself what the main (*Zweck*) of your message is and what results you expect from it.
3. Communication can take lots of forms. Ask yourself who needs to (*empfangen*) the message before you choose the appropriate form: one-to-one communication, conference, speech, presentation, etc.
4. Be (*einfach*), clear and brief. Keep to the main (*Thema*). Avoid details, technical terms, jargon and statistics. Tell them only what they need to know.
5. (*Prüfen Sie*) the facts. Wrong 'facts' are often the cause of disaster.
6. (*Treffen Sie*) the right tone. Who is your message (*gerichtet*) at? At experts or amateurs? Is your language appropriate? Is the timing right? Fine-tune the message accordingly.
7. Choose the right channel. Don't write a letter, if a telephone call will do the job. Use e-mail instead of faxes if you want to reach a group of people and expect a quick reaction.

Time for a smile

"Old" is when your wife says "Let's go upstairs and make love," and you answer, "Honey, I can't do both!"

Strike the right tone (see also Module 9)

Listeners want to be talked to. When you talk to an audience or to someone on the phone use spoken, not bookish language. Now here's an example:

Written message	Spoken message
Group words	**I, you, he, she, we**
Participants at meetings will experience how *tiring* it is to listen to a presentation that is read by the presenter.	*You* are in a meeting and the speaker doesn't talk to you. *He* reads his paper. And what happens? *You* doze off after a few minutes. *I* think *you* all know what *I* mean.
Reported speech	**Lively direct speech**
Dr Block informed me that he would introduce a modern communication system.	"You know what?" Dr Block said to me *the other day*, "I'm going to have this old communication system *replaced* by a modern one."
Abstract language	**Pictures and analogies**
Inflation is increasing.	Prices are sky-rocketing.

TASK 4: Compare and complete

inferior · regret · purchase · reduction
deliver · grant · deadline · supply

On the phone	In writing
Do we get the goods cheaper if we buy more than 1000?	Would you ________ us a ________ if we ____ in excess of 1000 items?
Can you let us have the goods by Tuesday?	Would it be possible *to* ________ the goods by Tuesday?
The goods were no good.	The goods were of ________ quality.
Sorry, but if you can't send us the goods on time we must find somebody else to get us the articles.	We ____________ to say that if it is impossible to keep the _______ we will be obliged to find an alternative ________.

The Psychologist's Corner

Body language: Our BEHAVE-Formula

You will never get a second chance to make a good impression. The first 30 minutes are the most important ones. Words aren't everything in a conversation. You can talk with your body by the way you dress, move, sit, stand and walk and that is even before you say a word. Only about 20 per cent of your message is conveyed by your words and about 40 per cent by your body language. And there is your facial expression, the tone of your voice, the distance you keep: everything contributes to the way we communicate with another person non-verbally. Our BEHAVE-Formula helps you to remember the golden rules of body language.

B	**Body**: Lean forward to encourage, lean or move away to discourage your partner from continuing.
E	**Eyes**: Don't stare at your partner. Keep eye contact for about three to five seconds before you look away. Glance down to the side and then back at your partner's face.
H	**Head**: Nod from time to time. It is a signal that you are listening and enjoying the conversation. A smile conveys warmth. **Hands**: Raise a finger to signal that you want to comment.
A	**Appearance**: You are what you wear. Your clothes are part of your body and speak a language of their own. **Attention**: Aim your attention at your partner. Don't fold your arms across your chest. This creates a barrier.
V	**Voice:** 40 percent of what you want to tell a person is expressed by tone, volume, speed and intonation. Breathe in through your nose. Speak in a calm, low voice at a rate of 100 to 120 words per minute.
E	**Ease**: Relax! Stand at ease and be at ease. It will make your partner feel comfortable. Keep a distance of at least one arm's length. When the conversation gets more personal you may move in up to 50 centimetres.

WORD AID

accordingly	*entsprechend*
appoint	*ernennen*
attempt	*Versuch*
break	*Pause*
breathe in	*einatmen*
concise	*kurz, prägnant*
convey	*mitteilen*
Cup	*hier: Fußball-Europameisterschaft*
doze off	*einschlummern*
emphasize	*betonen, hervorheben*
facial expression	*Gesichtsausdruck*
fag; a quick ~	*eine schnelle Zigarette*
forbid, forbade, forbidden	*verbieten*
gap	*Lücke*
gift of speech	*Gabe der Sprache*
goal; a common ~	*ein gemeinsames Ziel*
habit	*Gewohnheit*
height	*Höhe*
in addition to	*darüber hinaus, zusätzlich*
in excess	*mehr als*
increase	*steigen, vergrößern*
inferior	*minderwertig*
interpersonal skills	*Geschick im Umgang mit Menschen*
interruption	*Unterbrechung*
issue; serious ~	*ernsthaftes Thema, Problem*
jargon	*Fachjargon*
jealousy	*Eifersucht*
law	*Gesetz*
maintain	*aufrechterhalten, warten, pflegen*
mobile (phone)	*Handy*
nod	*nicken*
notepad	*Notizblock*

occasions; special ~	*besondere Anlässe*
pride	*Stolz*
provide	*sorgen für, liefern*
provide a room	*ein Zimmer bereitstellen*
purchase	*Kauf; kaufen*
purpose	*Zweck*
raise a finger	*einen Finger heben*
rate	*Geschwindigkeit, Tempo*
reduce	*verkleinern*
rules	*Regeln, Richtlinien*
size	*Größe*
suck	*saugen*
supply	*liefern; Vorrat*
support the majority	*die Mehrheit unterstützen*
switch off	*ausschalten*
tablet	*Tablette, Tafel*
take something on board	*etwas akzeptieren*
take something to the board	*etwas der Direktion berichten*
top down	*von oben*
topic	*Thema*
works council	*Betriebsrat*

Advice from the expert

Talk low, talk slow, and don't say too much.
John Wayne (1907–1979)

TALKING BODIES

Module 4

THE COMPLAINT

People might say one thing and mean another. However, the position of their body, the way they move, the expression on their faces, can show what they really feel about you. It's more a reflection of the soul. Researchers even say your body emits certain positive or negative chemicals which send messages to the person you're speaking to. Of course, this is difficult to describe in a dialogue. But we will try.

We focus on

- the art of reading body language
- handling complaints and
- how to make the angry customer your friend

The complaint

Busoom has its problems as we all do. In the last year, they have taken on more employees. Things must go more efficiently, especially the telephone communication. A representative from Telecrap is at a meeting with Hardman. Watch out for the body language hints!

Hardman (**H**), Mr Misfit (**M**) from Telecrap.

H: *(spreading his hands openly on the table top looking into Misfit's eyes*[1]) Well, we've had our problems with the telephone equipment and the software side, but we're glad you've managed to come along.

M: *(already feeling uncomfortable, he avoids eye contact with Hardman, he rubs his nose*[2]*)* Of course I am happy to be of any help I can with the telephone system. I can't imagine there's that much wrong, though. Perhaps there were user problems with the phones.

H: (*getting a little impatient*) Now come on, there were so many little problems and if there were user problems that is Telecrap's responsibility, too.

M: *(Misfit tears a piece of the notepad he is writing on*[3]*)* How do you come to that conclusion? We can be blamed for many things but not for user error.

H: (*smiling*) Aha! You haven't read the agreement. It says that within twenty-four hours of installation Telecrap must carry out a training workshop to explain and practise the use of the desk-phones. After all, there are a hundred thousand functions. Who in God's name can manage that especially after the age of forty? Where's your operational excellence?

M: (*rubbing his hands nervously*[4]) There must have been some misunderstanding. You say the workshop didn't take place at all. I'll just note that down. What exactly were the major problems with the equipment itself? (*fade out*)

1 The numbers in the text refer to the questions in the Analyst's Corner and to the answers in the Key.

H: (*ten minutes later*) ... and that brings me to the question of the software. Please look at the OHP transparency. What do you see?

M: A lot of statistics. It doesn't mean much to me. It's double-dutch!

H: I'll give you double-dutch. It shows how many calls came from outside and how many were actually answered. It was less than half of them. I can't run a business like that. That's no operational excellence!

M: (*has a hunched-up body position*[5]) That's all no problem at all. Again, in a way, it's a user problem. We have to train your staff to answer the phone.

H: (*with a raised voice*) I do believe you are not getting my message. The calls were not answered because nobody heard the phone ringing. Please wait! Before you interrupt me again. This does not mean my staff is deaf. It means the bells did not ring. It seems to me the bells don't actually ring very often at Telecrap. Now, ... (*fade out*)

WORKING with the language

TASK 1: Business phrases to remember

Ideen austauschen	______________ ideas
Angestellte einstellen	______________ employees
die Vereinbarung lesen	read the ______________
zu einer Entscheidung / einem Schluss kommen	______________ to a conclusion
ein Seminar durchführen	______________ a seminar
ein Geschäft leiten	______________ a business
jemandes Botschaft verstehen	______________ someone's message

The Analyst's Corner

TASK 2: Food for thought

1. What effect does Hardman achieve by spreading his hands on the table and looking into Misfit's eyes?
2. When and why do people avoid eye contact?
3. What might it mean when a person plays with things such as a piece of paper?
4. Why should you avoid rubbing your hands?
5. Misfit is hunched up. What does this suggest?

TASK 3: Interpreting body language

Let's do a little guesswork. What do you think these postures and gestures could mean? Of course, you can only read body language when you are part of the situation. Nevertheless, with this in mind try to match figures with letters.

1. Tent

A. impatience — Ungeduld
B. self-confidence — Sicherheit
C. doubt — Zweifel
D. fear — Furcht

2. Prayer

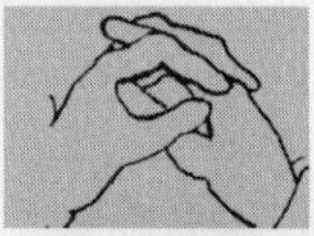

A. trust — Vertrauen
B. hope — Hoffnung
C. anxiety — Angst
D. suspicion — Misstrauen

3. Nose touch

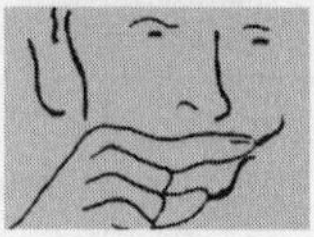

A. disdain — Verachtung
B. doubt — Zweifel
C. authority — Autorität
D. interest — Interesse

4. 'L' chin rest

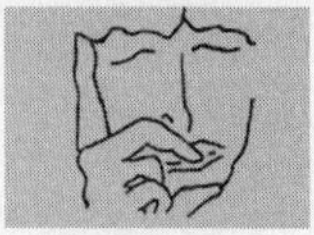

A. dislike — Abneigung
B. sympathy — Mitleid
C. animosity — Feindschaft
D. evaluation — Abschätzung

5. Arms up

A. reservation — Zurückhaltung
B. refusal — Ablehnung
C. sincerity — Aufrichtigkeit
D. certainty — Gewissheit

6. Lean forward

A. disagreement — Ablehnung
B. readiness — Bereitschaft
C. boredom — Langeweile
D. superiority — Überlegenheit

7. Thumbs out

A. shyness — Schüchternheit
B. resolution — Entschlossenheit
C. distrust — Misstrauen
D. authority — Autorität

Time for a smile

The Pithela Company manufactures baby food. They have been receiving a lot of complaints recently. So the manager in charge of quality control sends for the senior cook. "Some of our customers are under the impression that our puddings smell a bit mouldy. What's the problem?" – "Mouldy!? Look, young man," shouts the cook, "I produced first rate puddings for babies before you were born." – "Maybe so," replied the manager, "but why sell them now?"

MAGIC Squares

TASK 4: Balance the Magic Squares

If you match numbers and letters correctly all columns and rows will add up to the same number, 15. We've helped you a bit.

What might it mean if your opposite number does the following?

A. brushes a crumb off table	**B.** avoids eye contact	**C.** listens with closed eyes
D. plays with pencil	**E.** narrows his eyes	**F.** spreads hands on table
G. sits with legs crossed	**H.** passes hand over his watch	**I.** rubs his eyes

1. a sign of impatience
2. he / she dislikes you
3. a sign of insecurity
4. he / she doesn't agree with you
5. it's a sign of suspicion
6. he / she thinks you're lying
7. it's a sign of openness
8. he / she doesn't think much of you
9. a sign of nervousness, untruthfulness

A =	B =	C =
D =	E = 5	F =
G = 8	H =	I =

The Psychologist's Corner

Ten fool-proof steps to make an angry customer your friend

A customer who complains is like a bomb that may explode. So handle him with care and defuse him.

1. Take each complaint seriously. Remember, the customer is always right. Regard a complaint as a chance to improve your product or services.
2. Listen carefully. Don't interrupt.
3. Show sympathy! Don't give him the feeling that he is too stupid to handle the product or unable to read the instructions.
4. Ask polite questions until you have fully understood the problem and take notes. Wait for the answer before asking the next question.
5. Summarise the complaint. That shows him that you take it seriously.
6. Apologise, but do not admit any fault unless it is proved. Never put the blame on another person or department in your company.
7. Thank the customer for his criticism because he has helped you to save money in the future.
8. Offer solutions or compensation.
9. A customer who is complaining should never be told to call back. It's your duty to return the call.
10. If the complaint turns out to be unjustified, give him the opportunity to save face. Give him the feeling that he has taken part in solving the problem.

The next task gives you some ideas as to how to put theory into practice.

TASK 5: Words for defusing the angry customer

Can you complete these phrases? The first ones have been done for you.

1. Listen and ask

Was haben Sie für ein Problem?	May I ask what the problem is?
Würden Sie mir bitte Ihr Problem schildern?	Would you be so kind as to ___________ your problem?
Ich mache mir ein paar Notizen.	I'll make a few ___________.
Ich schreibe mir das gerade mal auf.	I'm just ___________ this down.

2. Show sympathy

Dies tut mir furchtbar Leid.	I'm awfully sorry to hear that.
Das ist wirklich ärgerlich.	That's really a nuisance.
Ich kann Ihre Unzufriedenheit verstehen.	I ___________ your dissatisfaction.
Ich kann mir Ihre Enttäuschung vorstellen.	I can imagine your ___________
Ich bin sicher, Ihre Reklamation ist gerechtfertigt.	I'm sure your complaint is ___________.

3. Apologise even if you are right

Die Unannehmlichkeiten, die Ihnen dadurch entstehen, tun mir außerordentlich Leid.	I'm extremely sorry for any inconvenience this has ________ you.
Bitte akzeptieren Sie unsere Entschuldigung.	Please _________ our apology.
Entschuldigen Sie bitte den Fehler unserer Rechnungsabteilung.	I do _________ for the error made by our accounts department.

4. Finding solutions

Wie können wir das wieder gutmachen?	How can we make up for the inconvenience?
Was erwarten Sie von uns in diesem Fall?	What do you __________ us to do in this case?
Wir ersetzen natürlich die Ware.	We'll of course ________ the article.
Oder hätten Sie lieber Ihr Geld zurück?	Or would you _______ to have your money ________?

5. Last words

Vielen Dank für Ihre Verbesserungsvorschläge.	Thank you for your suggestions to improve our product.
Es freut mich, dass es uns gelungen ist, die Angelegenheit zu regeln.	I'm pleased we managed to ______ it all out.
Ich bin froh, dass wir das Problem lösen konnten.	I'm relieved that we were able to ________ your problem.
Zögern Sie nicht, wieder anzurufen, sollte es erneut Probleme geben.	Don't ________ to call again should another problem crop up.

Typical American

An American businessman was invited by his English partner to a typical English fox hunt. When it was over his host took him aside and explained, "Look, when we first see the fox, we say 'Tallyho', not 'There goes the little son of a bitch.'"

WORD AID

WORD AID

apologise	*sich entschuldigen*
avoid eye contact	*Blickkontakt meiden*
blame someone for	*jemandem die Schuld geben für*
column	*Spalte*
come along	*vorbeikommen, besuchen*
compensation	*Entschädigung*
conclusion	*Schlussfolgerung; Abschluss*
deaf	*taub*
defuse	*entschärfen*
double-dutch	*unverständliches Kauderwelsch*
duty	*Pflicht*
equipment	*Ausrüstung*
etching	*(Kupfer-)Stich*
guesswork	*Raten, Erraten*
hint	*Hinweis*
hunch up	*sich zusammenkauern*
impatience	*Ungeduld*
improve a product	*ein Produkt verbessern*
interrupt	*unterbrechen*
match figures with letters	*Zahlen und Buchstaben in Übereinstimmung bringen*
message; you are not getting my ~	*Sie verstehen nicht, was ich sagen will*
mouldy	*schimmlig, verschimmelt*
narrow one's eyes	*die Augen zusammenkneifen*
notepad	*Notizblock*
OHP transparency	*Overheadfolie*
opportunity	*(günstige) Gelegenheit*
prove	*beweisen*
raised; with a ~ voice	*mit erhobener Stimme*
reflection of the soul	*Spiegelung der Seele*
responsibility	*Verantwortung*
row	*Reihe*

son of a bitch	*Hundesohn*
suspicion	*Misstrauen*
take notes	*Notizen machen*
take seriously	*ernst nehmen*
tear, tore, torn	*zerreißen*
though	*obwohl*
untruthfulness	*Unaufrichtigkeit*
user	*Anwender, Nutzer*
user error	*Anwendungsfehler*
wring one's hands	*seine Hände ringen*

Time for a smile

The greatest salesman in the world is the guy who brought a girl up to his apartment to see his etchings – and he sold her four etchings.

5 Module

WRITING FOR EFFECT (1)

THE LETTER OF COMPLAINT

In business there are some rules to follow as to the layout and the content. Poor old Hardman feels it is time to remind staff about this. He is not amused, but tries to keep his cool.

We focus on

- informal versus formal style
- layouting a business letter
- the language of letters

The letter of complaint

Hardman is always up to his neck in trouble. Perhaps he sets his targets too high – too many dreams about operational excellence. Anyway, once upon a time the following business fairy-tale happened. Poor old Hardman had to visit Japan on a business trip where he intended to take up contact to a supplier of special door frames. It was a difficult meeting, prices were high in Japan, especially as the Euro and the Deutschmark were so weak at that time. Hardman was worn out. He almost fell asleep as he was driving back to Tokyo Airport. Hardman (**H**) parked his rented car and went in the office to pay for it. The Office manager of Hearty Cars (**O**) greeted him. And then this:

O: So that'll be a total of £300 for the six days including insurance, petrol and mileage and so on.
H: Fine, do you take Misty Card?
O: We certainly do. Thank you. (*The office manager swipes it through the card machine. No result.*)
H: Is there a problem? My card is valid for another three months as you can see. Perhaps the magnetic strip is defective.
O: Well, it's not working. I'll just give Misty a quick phone call. (*Five minutes later*) It's a bit embarrassing, sir, but they told me your card is blocked. Perhaps you've gone into the red.
H: (*who was seeing red himself by now*) In the red? Good God. I'm the CEO of a multi-national company ...

And so it went on. Hardman was really angry. Fortunately, he had another card to get cash with but Hearty Cars didn't accept that card. In the end he missed his plane. Back in Britain he gave the details to his secretary and asked her to write a letter of complaint. Here's what she wrote:

Busoom Ltd
16, Warehouse Street, Deadbug

Dear Sir,
When I was in Tokyo on business my Misty card did not work.
I had no cash on me and found myself in a difficult situation as I owed the car rental company more than £300.
When they phoned your company you told him that my card had been stopped. I felt like a criminal and couldn't pay, so I missed my plane. What are you going to do about this?
Best wishes
H. Hardman

Well, at the end of the week Mr Hardman found a pile of papers on his desk waiting for his signature including this letter of complaint. Hardman had a red face. His revolver hand whipped out the live mobile at his waist. "Miss Dunno, please come here immediately." The girl had started at Busoom's two weeks earlier.

H: My dear Miss Dunno, communication is the key word. That means we want to tell somebody something in a clear way so that he or she gets the message. And writing a letter is a form of communication.

D: Have I done something wrong, Mr Hardman? I put everything down like you told me to. (*Tears in her eyes*).

H: (*who remembers his management training*) Never mind, never mind, Miss Dunno. Let's take it all as a learning experience. Let's look at a business letter, in this case a letter of complaint. There are two stages. Stage one, we make sure we design the letter in the correct formal way. Stage two, we try to write our sentences and paragraphs simply, clearly and in the correct sequence.

D: Didn't I do that, Mr Hardman?

H: Not exactly. Now look, here's a layout sheet which shows you what you have to include and in which place.

Business name
(often logo printed)
Sender's address

Your reference

Date
Recipient's name and address

Salutation (Dear Sirs)
Subject heading

[Main body]

Complimentary close

Sender's name
Sender's position / status

Enclosures

D: Oh, I didn't realise there were rules about all that. I'm sorry, Mr Hardman.
H: We've all got to learn. That's part of operational excellence.
D: Part of what, Mr Hardman?
H: Never mind! Remember stage two. We've got to state our reason for writing, we must stay calm, nothing emotional and hysterical. Present your facts at the beginning of the letter and then our request for action. (*fade out*)

Far from being a "don't know", Miss Dunno went back to her room and composed the following letter:

Busoom Ltd
16, Warehouse Street,
Deadbug

Card failure

4 December, 2001
Misty Card
Eppelhome Street,
Goatford

Dear Sirs,
I would like to express my dissatisfaction with your service. On November 15, of this year I went on a business trip to Japan. After my business was completed I drove in a rented car to Tokyo Airport. The rented car had to be paid for at their local agency. I attempted to pay for their service which totalled more than £300. My card did not function although it was still valid for the following three months. As a result they telephoned your headquarters in England. The answer they received was that my Misty Card had been blocked or cancelled or whatever you want. They refused to provide any further information. Moreover, any attempt by myself to find out what had happened was met with endless transfers of my call accompanied by metallic tones of Mozart's Eine Kleine Nachtmusik.
I missed my aeroplane and this cost £1,000. I was extremely inconvenienced by this trouble and feel I cannot rely on your services.
I expect from your side a reply to this letter within three days. I wish to know the reasons and, more importantly, I would like to discuss your compensation to my person for this disservice. Finally, I would like to mention that failure to comply with my wishes will result in the fact that this matter will be placed in the hands of my solicitors.

Yours sincerely
H. Hardman
CEO, Busoom Ltd

WORKING with the language

TASK 1: Business phrases to remember

Ziele zu hoch stecken	set ______________ too high
inklusive Versicherung	______________ insurance
Beschwerdebrief	letter of ______________
eine lehrreiche Erfahrung	a ______________ experience
seine Unzufriedenheit zum Ausdruck bringen	express one's ______________
eine Karte ist noch gültig	a card is still ______________
jemandes Wünschen entsprechen	______________ with someone's wishes
eine negative Auswirkung auf die Geschäftsbeziehung	a negative effect on the business ______________

The Analyst's Corner

TASK 2: Comparing the letters

We have built in five mistakes which you should not make in a formal letter. Can you find them?

The first letter

1. What did Mrs Dunno not do regarding the recipient?
2. Why is it important to show the logo?
3. What was basically wrong with the content?
4. What's wrong in the last lines?

The second letter

Look in the Key (page 221) for hints on how to write a good business letter.

TASK 3: Misty Card reacts

Read, choose and complete.

assure	regret	enclose
deficiency	control	incident
inconvenience	inadequacy	circumstances

Misty Card
Eppelhome Street
Goatford

24 May, 2001
Busoom Ltd
16, Warehouse Street,
Deadbug

Dear Mr Hardman,

We were indeed verry sorry to hear about the ______________ you had using our Misty Card.
After a thorough analysis of your case we are happy to _______ you that the disturbance was not caused by any __________ inherent in your Misty Card, but due entirely to ___________ beyond our ____________ . It seems that Japanese Telecom lines sometimes fail to cope with demands at peak hours.
I ___________ a cheque of £300 for the extra night you had to stay in Tokyo and very much ________ the inconvenience the ________ of Japanese computer lines has caused you. I also hope that this ________ will not have a negative effect on our future business relationship.

Yours faithfully
Carlos Tyson

TASK 4: The perfect letter

You get one point for each correct answer.
Check with the Key and get your mark.

A. The first and the last line

1. How do you start a letter to a man you do not know?
2. How do start a letter to a lady you do not know?
3. And what if you don't know if the recipient is male or female?
4. How do you start a letter to a company?
5. How do you end the above letters before you put your signature?
6. How do you end a letter that starts with *Dear Mr Bossy*?
7. When do you start it like this: *Dear Mrs Henriette Hornsucker*?

B. The first or the last sentence of the main body?

	first	last
8. we hope you will appreciate our position		
9. we regret to have you to tell that		
10. we should like to remind you that		
11. we look forward to hearing from you		
12. we wish to draw your attention to		

C. What type of letter do the sentences belong to?

13. If you have already sent a remittance please disregard this letter.
 A. a reminder
 B. a complaint
 C. an order

14. I would like to widen my experiences and work in a field with more responsibility.
 A. an enquiry
 B. an application
 C. an order

15. We thank your very much for your cooperation and guarantee you the strictest confidence.
A. a thank-you letter
B. an enquiry
C. an order

16. On the 14th June we placed an order for 120 electric motors, type M200 produced by you.
A. an enquiry
B. an order
C. a complaint

Complaints to customers are more formal

A reminder
Dear customer,
If I were you
And you were me,
a different story this would be.

If you were me
And I were you,
This bill would not be overdue.

Since I am I
And you are you,
Please send your cheque in
P.D.Q.*

* Pretty damn quick

MAGIC Squares

If you match numbers (business English) and letters (informal English) correctly all columns and rows will add up to the same number (**15**).

A. best wishes	**B.** sorry but	**C.** send us
D. no good	**E.** and another thing	**F.** buy more
G. we will do something	**H.** we need the following things	**I.** tell us how much

1. purchase in excess of
2. yours faithfully
3. the items listed below
4. we consider taking action
5. in addition to that
6. supply us with
7. we regret to say that
8. send us a quotation
9. of inferior quality

A =	B =	C =
D =	E =	F =
G =	H =	I =

WORD AID

application	*Bewerbung*
appreciate someone's position	*jemandes Standpunkt verstehen*
assure	*versichern*
attempt	*Versuch*
bill	*Rechnung*
blocked; a card is ~	*eine Karte ist gesperrt*
card failure	*defekte Karte*
CEO (chief executive officer)	*Vorstandsvorsitzender*
circumstances	*Umstände*
compensation	*Entschädigung, Wiedergutmachung*
complaint	*Beschwerde, Reklamation*
complimentary close	*Schluss-, Grußformel*
comply with someone's wishes	*jemandes Wünschen nachkommen*
compose a letter	*einen Brief formulieren*
confidence	*hier: Diskretion*
cope with	*fertig werden mit, gewachsen sein*
creditor	*Gläubiger*
current	*aktuell*
debts	*Schulden*
defective	*schadhaft, beschädigt*
deficiency	*Mangel*
dissatisfaction	*Unzufriedenheit, Unmut*
disservice	*miserabler Service; Bärendienst*
disturbance	*Störung*
draw attention to	*die Aufmerksamkeit lenken auf*
embarrassing	*peinlich*
enclose	*beilegen*
enclosures	*Anlagen*
enquiry	*Anfrage*
failure to comply with a wish	*Nichterfüllung eines Wunsches*
fairy-tale	*Märchen*
frame	*Rahmen*

get cash	*Bargeld erhalten*
inadequacy	*Unangepasstheit*
incident	*Vorfall*
inconvenience	*Unannehmlichkeit*
inconvenienced; be ~	*Unannehmlichkeiten haben*
insurance	*Versicherung*
intend	*beabsichtigen*
learning experience	*lehrreiche Erfahrung*
letter of complaint	*Beschwerdebrief*
live mobile phone	*eingeschaltetes Handy*
look forward to doing	*sich freuen zu tun*
magnetic strip	*Magnetstreifen*
main body	*Hauptteil*
neck; up to one's ~ in trouble	*tief in Schwierigkeiten stecken*
order	*Bestellung*
overdue	*überfällig*
owe someone something	*jemandem etwas schulden*
peak hours	*Stoßzeiten*
pile of papers	*Stoß Papier*
provide further information	*weitere Auskünfte geben*
quotation	*Angebot*
recipient	*Empfänger, Adressat*
red; be in the ~	*im Minus stehen*
reference	*Bezug, Aktenzeichen*
regret	*bedauern*
remind someone of something	*jemanden an etwas erinnern*
reminder	*Mahnung*
remittance	*Überweisung*
request for action	*Bitte um Veranlassung*
rule	*Regeln*
salutation	*Anrede, Gruß*
sequence	*Folge, Reihenfolge*
set targets too high	*Ziele zu hoch stecken*
solicitor	*Anwalt*
stage	*Stufe, Etappe, Schritt*

state a reason for	*einen Grund angeben für*
subject heading	*Themenzeile*
supplier	*Lieferant*
swipe a card through	*eine Karte durchziehen*
take up contact	*Verbindung aufnehmen mit*
total of £300	*Gesamtbetrag von 300 Pfund*
transfer of a call	*Weitervermittlung eines Anrufs*
valid	*gültig*
waist	*Taille*
worn; be ~ out	*erschöpft sein*

Incredible but true

A company sent a politely worded letter to a millionaire reminding him to pay the bill for his Rolls Royce. They received the following answer:

Dear Sirs,

I am used to dividing my creditors into three groups:
a) Those paid at once.
b) Those paid sometimes.
c) Those paid never.

I'm happy to inform you that I have promoted your company from group c to group b.

Yours sincerely
Ian McGregor

CONDUCTING AN INTERVIEW

THE APPLICANT

In Module 1 we met Mr Seaweed in a job interview with Mr Lost. We focussed on how Mr Lost failed to communicate with Seaweed. In this module we are indeed confronted by another job interview. This time, however, we should focus on the skills of Mr Seaweed as an interviewer. Here communication is written with a capital C.

Back in the world of Busoom, top management is searching for an Operations Manager to join the team of directors. Seaweed has to check him out. This is a top job, so he has to get it right.

We focus on

- what a CV should look like
- the open testimonial and how to read it
- how to conduct the interview
- how to be a good interviewee

The applicant

It's Wednesday morning. The interview is to begin at ten, but Seaweed is already there at 8 o'clock.[1] He's read Mr Bono's CV, but he wants an hour or so to think about it. Here's the communicative CV:

Curriculum Vitae: Charles Bono

Age: 35, married, 58 Albert Road, Chaddesden, Derby

EDUCATION

Secondary: *10GCE O levels; 3GCE A levels in English (A), Economics (B), Mathematics (C)*

Higher: *1988–1994*

University of Bradford, BA Economics (2:1)

Technical University of Berlin, Dip. Business Administration

Management Trainee: *1995–1997*

at the Door Company. Successfully participated in a rotation scheme which included working in the personnel department.

CAREER

The Door Company *1997–present*

The company supplies door systems to industrial customers in the region of northern England. Current turnover is DM 66 million. They are market leaders for revolving doors.

Technical Sales Manager *1998–present*

Responsible for sales and technical support for revolvers and sliding doors for 3 key accounts.

ACHIEVEMENTS

- *introduced new range of revolvers, exceeded targets by 20 %*
- *ensured product range was launched on time and budget was kept to*
- *planned and executed technical marketing programme*
- *completed initial feasibility study, approved by thc Board*
- *negotiated supplier agreement with European companies*

1 Numbers in text refer to Task 2 and Key to Task 2.

The interview

Mr Bono knocked at the door at 10 a.m. prompt. Seaweed stood up, walked over to Bono, shook his hand firmly (but didn't crunch it Schwarzenegger-style) and smiled[2].

S: How do you do? My name's Seaweed. I hope you had a comfortable journey. It wasn't difficult to find us, was it?
B: No, no problem at all.
S: Please take a seat. Can I offer you a cup of coffee?[3]
B: Thank you. Coffee would be fine.
S: Well, I've read your CV in detail and I'd like to say I'm very impressed[4]. You seem to have the sort of skills we're looking for. For example, I read here that you brought in a new range of revolvers and achieved 20 percent above targets. Could you tell me how you managed that?
B: Certainly. Well, I had a lot of support from good colleagues. We made a survey of the market and prepared technical quality brochures in advance. Then we contacted all our existing customers and mailed them. We offered them the new range at an introductory price, fifteen percent discount. The reaction was good.
S: So you had a good basis for business.
B: Yes, and I was able to work independently.
S: You mention in your CV that you also had to report to the Board.[5] What form did the report take?
B: Yes, I had to check the feasibility of outsourcing a department in our manufacturing division. The costs of a supplier compared with the costs of internal work. I did a computer presentation, I showed real costs and costs created internally.
S: Did you have any particular difficulties?
B: Yes, I found it hard to answer spontaneous questions from the Finance Director. I'm simply not specialized in that area.
S: I know what you mean. I'm not a technical person myself and I am very uncomfortable in technical things[6]. It's the same story. Just to change the topic. I noticed you have a gap in your CV. End of 1994.
B: That's right. I did a world tour.
S: Did you get any further qualifications during your tour?
B: If you mean "paper qualifications", no. But I attended some courses and did various jobs. (*fade out*)

WORKING with the language

TASK 1: Business phrases to remember

vom Vorstand genehmigt	____________ by the Board
Marktstudie in Auftrag geben	commission a _____ of the market
Einführungspreise anbieten	offer ____________ prices
das Thema wechseln	____________ the topic
ein Abkommen aushandeln	________ a supplier agreement
Marktführer für Türen	____________ leader for doors
Umsatzziele um 20 Prozent übertreffen	________ sales ________ by 20 percent
eine Produktreihe einführen	________ a product ________

The Analyst's corner

TASK 2: How do you see it?

1. Why is Seaweed already at the office at 8 o'clock?
2. What does Seaweed want to show by this behaviour?
3. What is the effect of Seaweed's offer of a cup of coffee?
4. Why does Seaweed mention he has read the CV?
5. What is your comment about this question? It's not about engineering.
6. What's Seaweed's intention by mentioning that he is not good at engineering and technical matters?

TASK 3: Do you know what a CV should look like?

	yes	no
The essential aim is to interest an employer so that he wants to know more about you.		
Your CV must include your date of birth.		
Mention evening classes and courses, even those you attended for personal reasons.		
You need not state the reason why you left your former companies.		
Is this sentence is ok?: 'My responsibilities included training staff in new customer-care procedures.'		
Is this sentence is ok?: 'Successfully trained staff in new customer-care procedures' (see page 13).		

A. The aim of a CV

1. A CV provides a summary of your education, training and work experience to date in the space of one, possibly two, sides of A4 paper.
2. A good CV conveys all the reasons why an employer should want to know more about you. It excites interest by showing clearly that you are someone who can offer skills and personal qualities.
3. The essential aim of your CV is to interest an employer sufficiently to open the door to the next stage of the recruitment process. CVs alone won't get you a job, but they must beat off most of the competition, which can be fierce for some jobs.

B. The content of the CV

Personal details

1. Name, marital status, address and telephone number are sufficient.
2. If the advertisement specifies an age limit, include your date of birth.

Work experience

1. State the period during which you worked for each employer (month and year).

2. The reason for leaving is not normally included on CVs.
3. Give the name of each company and its location (not full address); next put your job title.
4. Itemise your main responsibilities and duties; give most details for the most recent employers.
5. It's essential to include your achievements that are relevant to the job you're applying for.
6. Professional memberships, etc.
7. Include any other accomplishments relevant to your profession, such as special awards or distinctions.

Education and training

1. Give details of any training or course of study since leaving formal education.
2. Name of college or university and years of attendance, qualification and subject.
3. Don't include evening classes and courses attended for personal interests unless they are directly relevant to the job.

C. The language of the CV

Your CV should contain short, abbreviated descriptions and not necessarily full sentences. Follow these guidelines:

1. Avoid the first person *I*.
2. Eliminate as many words as you can (like *the* and *that*), unless they change the meaning or readability.
3. Try to start each item with a verb – this makes the point that you're actively doing and achieving things in your work.
4. Use adverbs to convey how the achievements were fulfilled, instead of '*My responsibilities included training* staff in new customer-care procedures' change to '*Successfully trained* staff in new customer-care procedures'.
   Use the winners, not the losers (see Module 1, page 13).

The Psychologist's Corner

TASK 4: The open testimonial and how to read it

Apart from your CV the personnel manager expects testimonials from your former employers. In many countries there is a regulation which says that an employee cannot be given a testimonial which is formulated in a negative way. But since employers want to know the truth about an employee, personnel departments have worked out a code. Formulations are used which have different meanings in the background.

Quiz time: What do these sentences really mean, A or B?

1. Mr B. has always managed well with his superiors.
   A. He always does good work for his bosses.
   B. He adapts to his superior at any price.
2. He always deals with his work in a right and proper way.
   A. He does not have any initiative, he is a typical bureaucrat.
   B. He is a careful worker, hardly makes mistakes.
3. Mr B. is a sociable colleague.
   A. Most of his colleagues like him.
   B. He prefers talking and drinking to working.
4. He has a sense of what is essential.
   A. He has a strongly developed sense of target-orientation.
   B. He does not pay attention to detail.
5. He is diligent and knows how to sell himself.
   A. He blows up his importance.
   B. He is hard-working and knows how to present himself well.
6. He always tries to do his best to complete his tasks.
   A. He does his best but his best is never good enough.
   B. He has the right attitude to his work.
7. He has the ability to motivate colleagues in a target-oriented way.
   A. He is too much of an individual.
   B. He is a good leader of people.
8. He always fulfilled our expectations.
   A. His performance was unsatisfactory the whole time.
   B. He worked regularly and in a successful way.

TASK 5: Can you create the right atmosphere?

When a candidate arrives for an interview he or she is probably nervous. The good interviewer will know how to put the candidate at ease.

Greetings

Guten Tag. Mein Name ist Bright.	How ____________? My name's Bright.
Freut mich, Sie kennen zu lernen, Herr Bright.	Pleased to _________ you, Mr Bright.
Ganz meinerseits.	The pleasure _________.

Icebreakers

Haben Sie unsere Firma gleich gefunden?	_________ find our company straight away?
Dank Ihrer genauen Beschreibung hatte ich keine Probleme.	___________ any trouble thanks to your clear instructions.
Nehmen Sie doch bitte Platz.	Please ______________.
Darf ich Ihnen etwas zum Trinken anbieten? Kaffee, Tee oder sonst etwas?	_____ I _______ you something to drink? Coffee, tea or something else?
Ich nehme das Gleiche wie Sie.	_________ the same as you.
Ich schlage vor, wir lassen die Förmlichkeiten beiseite.	I _________ we drop the formalities.

Time for a smile

There was a fellow who applied for a job as a press aid to the Conservative party. Not long after he submitted his application, he received word from the party leader.

"Your letter of application is full of exaggerations, distortions, half-truths and lies. Can you start work on Monday?"

Communicator's Corner

How to conduct the interview

Recruiting the right man or the right woman today isn't easy. Often you have to live with the result for a long time. It's like marriage and the chances of success are about the same. It all depends on your skills as an interviewer.

1. Take time to read the interviewee's CV carefully.
2. Take brief notes; expand them later.
3. Get the applicant to enlarge on the facts given in the CV.
4. Watch out for the applicant embellishing the facts.
5. Don't ask questions which cause yes / no answers.
6. Take your time and listen patiently.
7. Give the candidate the chance to ask questions.
8. What are the applicant's interpersonal skills?
9. Will he or she fit into your team?

How to be a good candidate

1. Collect information about the company, its products and problems.
2. Act as if you want the job and when asked explain why.
3. Give concrete examples of your work performance.
4. Be prepared to answer questions about decisions you took, risks you had to take, problems you solved.
5. Prepare your answers as to your personal objectives. How do you see yourself in five years?
6. Be honest.
7. Have questions ready to ask the interviewer.

Food for thought

The most important thing in an interview is to hear what isn't being said.

TASK 6: Beef up your word power

Business English to take with you before leaving the chapter

1. You interview candidates, applicants or ______________
2. If they are good you hire, employ or____________ them.
3. What is the verb? You can ______________ notes, time, decisions and risks.
4. If a candidate ______________ the facts he is not honest.
5. Expanding notes means
   A. typing **B.** completing **C.** rewriting them
6. Enlarging on facts in one's CV means
   A. changing **B.** embellishing **C.** commenting on the facts

WORD AID

abbreviate	*abkürzen*
accomplishment	*Talent, Leistung, Vollkommenheit*
achievement	*Leistung*
advance; in ~	*im Voraus*
age limit	*Altersgrenze*
approved by the Board	*vom Vorstand genehmigt*
attend evening classes	*Abendkurse besuchen*
attendance (of a university)	*Besuch, Studienzeit*
brief notes	*kurze Notizen*
business administration	*Betriebswirtschaft*
change the topic	*das Thema wechseln*
comfortable journey	*angenehme Reise*
common ground	*Gemeinsamkeiten*
contain	*enthalten, beinhalten*
crunch someone's hand	*jemandes Hand zerquetschen*
curriculum vitae	*Lebenslauf*

customer-care procedures	*Kundendienstmaßnahmen*
digest	*verdauen, verarbeiten*
distortion	*Verzerrung, Verdrehung*
embellish the facts	*Fakten schönfärben*
essential	*wesentlich, wichtig*
exaggeration	*Übertreibung*
expand notes	*Notizen erweitern, ergänzen*
experience to date	*aktueller Stand der Berufserfahrung*
fail to communicate	*Verständigungsschwierigkeiten haben*
feasibility study	*Machbarkeitsstudie*
fierce competition	*scharfe Konkurrenz*
gap	*Lücke*
impressed	*beeindruckt*
include	*mit einschließen*
independently; work ~	*unabhängig, selbständig arbeiten*
introductory price	*Einführungspreis*
item	*Punkt, Thema, Artikel*
itemise	*einzeln aufführen*
negotiate	*verhandeln, aushandeln*
objectives	*Ziele*
outsourcing	*Leistungen durch Vertragsfirmen*
particular difficulties	*besondere Schwierigkeiten*
performance	*Leistung*
press aid	*Assistent des Pressesprechers*
promote	*befördern; fördern*
range	*Reihe, Palette*
readability	*Lesbarkeit*
recent	*kürzlich*
recruitment process	*Vorgehensweise bei Neueinstellung*
relevant to	*wichtig, wesentlich für*
revolver, revolving door	*Drehtür*
rotation scheme	*Rotationssystem (für Trainees)*
senior executive	*leitender Angestellter*
sliding door	*Schiebetür*
sociable	*gesellig*
submit an application	*eine Bewerbung einreichen*

sufficient(ly)	*aus-, hinreichend*
superior	*Vorgesetzter*
supplier agreement	*Liefer(anten)vertrag*
supply	*liefern*
support	*Unterstützung*
survey of the market	*Marktstudie*
take trouble with someone	*sich um jemanden bemühen*
target	*Ziel*
target-oriented	*zielbewusst*
testimonial	*Beurteilung, Zeugnis*
various jobs	*verschiedene Tätigkeiten*

Time for a smile

The director of the board wanted to promote one of his junior managers to the senior executive level. He handed out a questionnaire to the possible candidates. One of the questions was: "Do you believe that you have executive potential?"
One of the candidates wrote in answer: "I think I have executive potential because I like to be alone, I never get lonely, and I would like to work in a private office on my own, and I don't care if people say bad things about me."

THE COMMUNICATIVE PRESENTATION

Module 7

CAUGHT IN A REVOLVER

Communication is a big word. It covers many situations. Basically a person has something to say and wants to get his message over to another person. In this case Ramsch has to give a message to a group of people using the vehicle of a presentation to do it. Judge for yourself whether he manages it.

We focus on

- how to prepare a presentation
- checklists for presenters
- handy phrases to structure a presentation and
- on style

Caught in a revolver

Busoom was drifting along peacefully. There wasn't much innovation although Hardman was trying to introduce it where he could. Most often he heard the following from his staff: "That's the way things were in the past. It works quite well. Why should we change anything?" It made his blood boil. This is not to say that there were no innovations at Busoom. Actually they had designed a new revolving door and the launch was to be in a few weeks. Hardman had great hopes of it and had invited representatives from his key customers to an informal presentation. Time was short. Hardman phoned Mr Ramsch, Head of Production.

H: David, can you present the gist of the news about our R 301 to a selected audience?

R: Sure, no sweat (*he'd lived in the States for two years*). When?

H: Tomorrow at 11 a.m.

R: That's real short notice, but I'll get it together. (*Hardman was anxious. He couldn't be there himself and he had a bad feeling.*)

H: Make sure you do it well! It's an important cross-section of our key customers.

That evening Ramsch had a quick look through his documentation. It was new for him, but he decided to do it spontaneously. Time was too short. What could he do to make it as simple as possible with less work for himself? "Yes, we'll have a short introduction and then take them to our demonstration revolving doors."[1] The next day in the conference room, thirty people from Busoom's customer base are gathered together, eager to hear what Mr Ramsch has to say:

R: ... so Ladies and Gentlemen or should I say Gentlemen, since today we have no Ladies present, we didn't have them in the past either, but I hope we'll have a few in the future, ha, ha[2]! On behalf of our company I'd like to welcome you all. We appreciate that you're sacrificing one day of your valuable time to get to know our latest technological achievement. My name is David Ramsch and I'm glad to

---

1 The numbers refer to the questions in the Analyst's Corner and to the answers in the Key.

have the chance to present what I think is a particularly fine piece of hardware ... Well, to come to the point (*grunting from the back row: "it's certainly time you did that"*) ... to get to the point, our revolver is really novel. It does special new things. As it were, it reaches the parts other doors can never reach, to quote a famous lager spot on the TV. (*Irritated voice from the audience. "Hey, can you get on with it? We've got other appointments as well, you know." Ramsch began to feel nervous.*)

R: Yes, of course. Well, would you look here at the flipchart – and don't hesitate to interrupt me when you have a question. I'll just sketch up the main novelties on the R 301 (*which Ramsch then proceeded to do. He was pretty quick, but it was a complicated task. A voice from the audience. "Mr Ramsch, I'm sorry, you're in your own way. We can't see it from here." Another voice, "and by the way, the diagram's too small. We can't see the details"* [3]).

Finally, Ramsch was finished. He described the 301 pointing to the new features with his finger (which unfortunately was not long enough). He glanced at his watch[4]. He was already fifteen minutes over time.

R: Ladies and Gentlemen, if you would all follow me, I'll show you the revolver in action. It's in the production area, a five minute-walk from here.

Ramsch quickly walked to the door of the conference room. It was the 'Busoom Automatic Slider'. The group of buyers followed obediently. Ramsch walked to the door which should have opened as soon as the sensor detected him. Of course it didn't, Ramsch kept walking, couldn't stop in time and banged his nose on the glass, his spectacles fell off and onto the floor. It was too late to stop himself from treading on them. The door was finally opened from outside by the company cook.

R: If you'll all follow me now, these little things cannot disturb a great spirit.[5]

They walked on for five minutes and arrived in front of the 'revolver' in the production department, a magnificent example of a door, of the type you find on the front of famous hotels and department stores.

R: Just watch! You remember, I described the two buttons on the door panel which you press when you're in trouble. I'll just pass through. See, it's effortless.

Ramsch walked through into his segment of the door which glided gently in front of him, and stopped after a yard or so. Ramsch who doesn't like to be in small places turned red.

R: Ha, ha. An emergency. (*Ramsch gesticulated at the leader of the pack.*) Press the emergency button! Thank you.

The willing victim (the Purchasing Manager of Auldit) pressed the button and was immediately met by a bunch of sparks. He jumped backwards as if he'd been stung by a bee. "Hey, I say, if this is your idea of a joke. Well, I'm not amused."
Mr Ramsch didn't answer. He was too busy banging on the soundproof glass. Finally, hours later the door moved again. Mr Ramsch was all alone in the company.

WORKING with the language

TASK 1: Business phrases to remember

Neuerungen einführen	___________ innovations
eine neue Drehtür planen	___________ a new revolving door
die Markteinführung sollte in einer Woche sein	the ___________ was to be in a week
ein wichtiger Querschnitt unserer Kundschaft	an important _____-______ of our customers
jemandem die Drehtür in Aktion zeigen	show someone the revolver _____ _______
den Tagungsort inspizieren	to inspect the ___________

How to thank the presenter

Thank you, Mr Smith, you have presented a series of good, new ideas. Unfortunately the good ideas weren't new and the new ideas weren't any good.

The Analyst's Corner

TASK 2: What went wrong?

1. When Ramsch went home the evening before the presentation what did he do wrong?
2. What is Ramsch's mistake at this point in the presentation and why is it not appropriate?
3. What's the criticism of Mr Ramsch using the flipchart? What's the background to all this?
4. "He glanced at his watch." What is the problem with the time here?
5. Ramsch tried to lead the audience out of the conference room. The revolving door did not function. What should Ramsch have done here?

The Communicator's Corner

The Perfect Presenter's Checklists

Before you start drafting the presentation you should have a clear idea who you are going to talk to and what they want to hear.

CHECKLIST 1: Adapting to the audience

1. How can I find out more about my audience? (by asking the organiser etc.)
2. Is it a heterogeneous or homogeneous audience?
3. What are the education, background, functions of my listeners?
4. Will there be specialists among the listeners?
5. What age group do they belong to?
6. Will they need a coffee break?
7. Will it be an all male audience or will there be women, too?

8. What do they already know about my subject?
9. What do they expect of my speech?
10. How can I compliment my audience?
11. Have I adapted the style of my speech to their background?
    - the length of my sentences?
    - the choice of my words?
    - the figures of speech?
    - the jokes?
12. Will they agree with me or will there be resistance?
13. Which media are best suited for my speech?
    - flipchart?
    - OHP?
    - slides?
    - videos?
    - handouts?
14. Find out how other people feel about your topic.

CHECKLIST 2: Drafting the presentation

1. How long am I supposed to speak?
2. What is my purpose? Do I want to
    - inform?
    - entertain?
    - persuade?
3. How do I appeal to the audience? Shall I appeal to
    - logic?
    - emotions?
    - needs?
    - fears?
4. What is going into the body of my speech?
    - comparisons?
    - examples?
    - facts?
    - statistics?
    - testimony by authorities?

5. Which counter-arguments will I have to disarm?
6. How am I going to organise the parts of my speech?
   - chronologically?
   - by cause and effect?
   - by problem and solution?
   - from weaker arguments to stronger arguments?
7. Do I have a good opening?
   - proverb?
   - joke?
   - anecdote?

CHECKLIST 3: Writing the outline

KISS, don't KILL!*

1. Use spoken not written English. When preparing your presentation, don't copy from catalogues or specifications. They are written English.
2. Brevity is the soul of wit. What is your message? Be selective.
3. Select the most effective arguments.
4. Present your weak arguments first, your strong ones last.
5. Weaken the strongest counter-argument first, the weakest last.
6. Restate your arguments at the end.
7. Supply your arguments with good examples, facts and figures.
8. Don't overload your presentation with figures.
9. Take into account possible objections from the audience.
10. Paint the future bright.
11. Appeal for action.
12. Don't ever lose sight of what you want them to do.
13. Check if your outline is clear so that it supports you through the presentation.
14. Invite questions from the audience. Estimate about 15 extra minutes.
15. Think of a light conclusion.
16. Get feedback. Use a tape recorder to rehearse your presentation. Do it in front of a mirror.

*KISS: keep it short, simple; KILL: keep it lengthy, long-winded

CHECKLIST 4: Explore the venue

1. Visit the presentation venue in advance.
2. If this is not possible ask the organizer to send a detailed floorplan showing all the facilities.
3. Check the acoustics. Ask an assistant to stand at several different points to find out if he can hear you at the back of the room.
4. Check whether everybody will be able to see you and the screen or the flipchart.
5. Does the layout of the room (horseshoe, circles, classical classroom ...) suit your purpose and the size of the audience?
6. Provide a table for the audience to collect the handouts after the presentation.
7. Make sure that the power points and dimmers are within reach. Check whether you need extension leads.
8. Position refreshments at the rear of the venue to avoid distractions.

CHECKLIST 5: The OHP

1. Don't use more transparencies than you have fingers.
2. Don't put more words or graphics on a transparency than you would on a T-shirt. Seven lines (plus / minus two) is the limit.
3. Each line should have between seven and fourteen syllables.
4. Don't sit – stand, but don't stand in front of the screen.
5. Don't turn your back on the audience.
6. Don't talk to your transparency, the screen or to the OHP – talk to the audience.
7. Don't point with your hand. Use a transparent pointer or a biro.
8. Don't hold the pointer. Place it on the transparency, otherwise the trembling of your hand will be amplified. A small movement becomes a big and hectic movement on the screen.
9. Don't tap the transparency with your pencil or your pointer.
10. By the way, the first six rules also apply to flipcharts.

What not to say to the presenter

I'll never forget your presentation – although I'll keep trying.

Phrases for presenters step by step

TASK 3: Introduce yourself

Meine Name ist David Ramsch.	My name is David Ramsch.
Ich bin seit drei Jahren in der Drehtürbranche.	I _____ _____ in the revolving door business ____ three years.
Ich kenne Ihre Probleme, da ich wie die meisten von Ihnen Verkaufsmanager gewesen bin.	I ______your problems _______ I was a sales manager _______ most of you.
Ich bin auf diesem Gebiet auch nicht mehr Fachmann als Sie.	I'm ____ _______ expert in this field _______ you are.

How not to introduce yourself

Before I get to the work at hand, let me say that to be chosen as presenter is more than an honour. We had to draw lots – I lost!

TASK 4: Welcome the audience

Im Namen unserer Firma möchte ich Sie alle zu unserer Vorführung begrüßen.	____ _______ of our company I'd like to welcome you all here to our demonstration.
Wir freuen uns sehr, Sie heute bei uns zu haben.	We're very ___________ to have you _____ us today.
Ich bin sehr froh, dass wir Gelegenheit haben, über diese Angelegenheit zu diskutieren.	I'm so glad that we have the ___________ to ___________ this matter.
Ich bin Ihnen dankbar, dass Sie eine Stunde Ihrer wertvollen Zeit opfern, um mir zuzuhören.	I ___________ that you're sacrificing one hour of your _________ time to listen to me.

How to compliment the audience

After such a warm reception I can hardly wait to hear myself speak.

TASK 5: Announce the purpose of the presentation

Das Thema meiner Präsentation ist der Durchbruch auf dem Gebiet der Schiebetüren.	The _________ of this presentation is a breakthrough ___ ____ _______ of sliding doors.
Ich versuche, Ihnen einen Überblick über unsere Dienstleistungen zu geben.	I'm trying to give you an ________ ___ our company's services.
In meiner Präsentation versuche ich, neue Wege bei der Installation von Türen zu erläutern.	In my presentation I'___ ___ _____ to explain a new way of installing doors.
Zögern Sie nicht, mich zu unterbrechen, wenn Sie eine Frage haben.	Don't ________ to ________ me when you have a question.

How to break the ice

Before I begin my speech I'd like to warn you that I'm suffering from a severe handicap – I'm sober.

TASK 6: Explain the structure

Meine Präsentation besteht aus drei Hauptteilen.	My presentation will be in three _____ _____ .
Ich werde die drei Stufen unseres SX1 darlegen.	I'll be ___________ the three ______________ of our SX1.
Zu Beginn darf ich Ihnen die Kontrolltafel zeigen.	To _______ _____, let me show you the control panel.
Zuerst möchte ich ... Zweitens können wir ... Und ich will mit ... schließen.	________, I'd like to ... Secondly, we can ... And I'll ___________ with ...

Advice from the expert

The best audience is one that is intelligent, well-educated and a little drunk.
Alben Barkley

TASK 7: Conclusion

Abschließend möchte ich sagen, dass ...	I'd like to round off ___ ________ ...
Lassen Sie mich mit den Worten schließen ...	____ __ _______ by saying that ...
Ich möchte mit der Feststellung schließen, dass ...	I'd like to ___________ by ________ that ...
So, das war's für heute. Vielen Dank für Ihre Aufmerksamkeit, meine Damen und Herren.	So that was it ____ _________ . Thank you for your __________ , Ladies and Gentlemen.

Time for a smile

At the end of a presentation, the chairman rose and said, "Your presentation has not left me any the wiser."
The presenter retorted, "Perhaps not wiser, sir, but better informed."

A question of style

Use spoken English instead of written English. Most people prepare their presentations in writing. The result is more often like a chapter from a handbook rather than natural speech. Here's an example:

Avoid written style	Use spoken English
A, B, C	**A and B and C**
Our revolving door, the dimensions of which are two metres by two metres, represents the most sophisticated equipment on the market for a price which is unbeatable.	Our revolver is really state of the art *and* your whole family can comfortably walk through it at one go *and* you won't find better value for money.
third person: he, they	**first or second person: I, you**
The user of traditional revolving doors will have *encountered* disagreeable *failures.*	*You* know when *you* buy one of these revolvers of type BB – i. e. Before Busoom – *you* might be in for an adventure.
abstract phrases	**call a spade a spade**
We have *evidence* that ordinary revolving doors have been the cause of considerable *inconvenience* to families especially in case of *misapplications* by minors.	*I* suppose *we*'ve all heard that sort of unpleasant surprise. You buy a cheap revolver and then your son plays merry-go-round with it and finds himself trapped and has to wait till a mechanic gets him out again. A nightmare!

WORD AID

advert	*Werbung, Annonce*
appeal to fears	*Ängste ansprechen*
apply to	*hier: gelten für*
appointment	*Verabredung, Termin*
audience	*Publikum*
avoid distractions	*Ablenkung vermeiden*
body of a speech	*Hauptteil einer Rede*
brevity is the soul of wit	*in der Kürze liegt die Würze*
bunch of sparks	*Funkenregen*
cause and effect	*Ursache und Wirkung*
collect	*abholen, sammeln*
come to the point	*zur Sache kommen*
concerned; be ~ with	*betreffen, befasst sein mit*
cross-section	*Querschnitt*
detect	*feststellen, entdecken*
disarm an argument	*ein Argument entkräften*
draw lots	*losen*
drift along peacefully	*ruhig dahintreiben, in ruhigem Fahrwasser sein*
emergency	*Notfall*
emphasise	*betonen, hervorheben*
estimate	*schätzen*
facilities	*Einrichtungen*
fate	*Schicksal*
feature	*Merkmal*
figures of speech	*rhetorische Mittel, Stilfiguren*
gist	*das Wesentliche, Kernpunkt*
grunt	*brummen, murren, grunzen*
honour	*Ehre*
irritated	*gereizt*
key-accounts	*Hauptkunden*
launch (of a product)	*Markteinführung*

male	*männlich*
met, be ~ by	*abgeholt werden von*
needs	*Bedürfnisse*
novelty	*Neuheit, Neuerung*
objection	*Einwand, Widerstand*
panel	*Schalttafel*
persuade	*überzeugen, überreden*
proceed to do	*sich anschicken zu tun, übergehen zu*
proverb	*Sprichwort*
purpose	*Zweck, Ziel*
quote	*zitieren*
rear; at the ~	*hinten, im hinteren Teil*
reception	*Empfang*
rehearse	*proben*
restate	*wiederholen*
retort	*erwidern*
revolving door	*Drehtür*
rise, rose, risen	*sich erheben; (Preise) steigen*
set into motion	*in Bewegung setzen*
screen	*Bildschirm, Projektionsfläche*
seal a fate	*ein Schicksal besiegeln*
selective	*wählerisch*
sober	*nüchtern*
soundproof	*schalldicht*
specifications	*technische Beschreibung*
supply	*liefern; hier: ausstatten*
emphasize	*betonen, hervorheben*
sweat; no ~!	*kein Problem!*
take into account	*berücksichtigen, Rechnung tragen*
this cannot disturb a great spirit	*das kann einen großen Geist nicht aus der Fassung bringen*
transparency	*Overheadfolie*
venue	*Schauplatz, Tagungsort*

PHONING EFFECTIVELY

Module 8

HIT OR MISS ON THE PHONE

Communication turns up everywhere. A visiting card communicates something. A telephone call is also a type of visiting card. Actually it is even more vital because it can be the first direct contact with the customer. Some people using the phone on behalf of the company do not seem to realise this. The result is poor communication.

We focus on

- telephone phrases
- telephone etiquette
- telephone psychology

Hit or miss on the phone

Well, if there's one thing that gets on Hardman's nerves, it's the whole question of the telephone. Whether it's leaving a message, finding the right person, getting connected or simply finding someone to answer the phone it's a disaster. "No operational excellence!" Hardman decided to test the situation for himself. "I'll ring our operator and have her put me through to the Sales Supervisor." The phone rang five, ten, fifteen times. No answer. Hardman banged the receiver down on the phone. "I'll have their heads. I could be a customer. Don't they want to keep their jobs?"
He tried again. After ten rings a bored sounding voice: "Hello. Can I help you?"[1]
"Help me?!" thundered Hardman. "You'd better think how you can help yourself to keep your job. I could've been a customer. And you didn't greet me correctly[2]. Why didn't you answer five minutes ago?"
The operator felt angry. "I had to take a message for somebody."
"Oh, did you? Put me through to the Sales Supervisor, please."
Sensual music growled in Hardman's ear. "Jesus. Who chose the Can Can? Are we a strip club?"
Thirty seconds later the operator's voice came on. "He's not at his desk. Please try again later." The click of the operator cutting Hardman off went off like a bomb in his ear. Hardman turned bright red.

Well, dear reader, as you saw in the text a few things went wrong in the communication. But this was by no means everything. Look what happened in this dialogue between Ellen Cocky (**C**) and Hardman (**H**) from Busoom.

C: (*on the phone*) Hi, my name is Cocky from Combinations. I think you've received the information I sent you.[3]
H: Information? Sorry, what was the name? Connections?
C: Combinations. I'm ringing on behalf of Dr Bossybitch.[4]
H: I don't know Dr Bissybotch from Adam.

---

1 The numbers refer to the questions in the Analyst's Corner and to the answers in the Key.

C: You know, it's about our special English training for presentations and meetings.

H: Aha. Now I'm beginning to get the message. But you're speaking to the wrong person[5]. I'm the CEO. Mr Seaweed, our Personnel Director, is responsible for all our training. I'll put you through to him.

Let's start with a smile

Jim Turner has been trying for days to get through to Bill Gates. At last he got his secretary.
"My name is Jim Turner and I'm with the Human Resource Department at the Acme Company. I'm calling to check on a reference given to us by a job applicant. This applicant said that Mr Gates was a close personal friend. I'd like Mr Gates to get back to me about this individual and be so kind as to answer a few questions ... "
"Well, let's see," said the secretary and browsed through Mr Gates' agenda. "I'll add your name to Mr Gates' list. You're right behind Steven Spielberg, George W. Bush, Prince Charles and the Pope. And thank you for calling Microsoft."

WORKING with the language

TASK 1: Telephone phrases to remember

Was kann ich für Sie tun?	________ I ________ you?
Ich rufe im Auftrag von Herrn X an.	I'm ringing __ ________ of Mr X
Verbinden Sie mich bitte mit Herrn Y.	Please _______ me _______ to Mr Y.
Er ist leider nicht an seinem Platz.	I'm afraid he's not __ his ______.
Könnten Sie Herrn Y etwas ausrichten?	Could you _________ a message for Mr Y?
Oh, man hat mich aus der Leitung geschmissen / getrennt.	Oh, they've _______ me ________.

The Analyst's Corner

TASK 2: Would you have got it right?

1. The phone has rung more than five times. What must the operator do first when she answers the phone?
2. What should the correct greeting have been from the operator?
3. What's missing in Cocky's first few sentences to a new customer/telephone partner?
4. What went wrong here?
5. What is the mistake here in the background to the conversation?

The Communicator's Corner

TASK 3: Telephoning effectively

The first two phrases of each step have been done for you. Try the rest.

1. Answering the phone

Living Models. Guten Morgen. Sie wünschen?	Living Models. Good morning. Can / May I help you?
Ruver Ltd. Guten Tag. Kann ich Ihnen helfen?	Ruver Ltd. Hello. Can I be of help?
Guten Tag. Was kann ich für Sie tun?	Hello. How __________ you?

Time for a smile

A caller who dials the wrong number will call a second time as soon as you have returned to your living room and made yourself comfortable.

2. Tell them who you are

Hier ist Jack Brown. Guten Morgen.	Jack Brown here. Good morning.
Hier spricht Tom Smith von der Firma Ruver.	This is Tom Smith of Ruver speaking.
Spreche ich mit Herrn X?	Hello? __________ Mr X?

3. Identifying the caller

Würden Sie mir bitte Ihren Namen nennen?	Could you give me your name, please?
Wen darf ich bitte melden?	Who shall I say is calling?
Darf ich um Ihren Namen bitten?	May I _______ who is calling?
Entschuldigen Sie, ich habe Ihren Namen nicht richtig verstanden.	I'm sorry, sir. I didn't quite ______ your name.

4. Who do you want to speak to?

Grüß Gott. Ist Herr Jones da? Ich würde gerne mit ihm sprechen.	Hello, is Mr Jones there? I'd like to speak to him.
Geben Sie mir bitte Apparat 344.	Could I have extension 344, please?
Geben Sie mir bitte Ihre Verkaufsabteilung.	Could you _______ me _______ to your sales department, please?

5. Asking what it's about

Was ist der Grund Ihres Anrufs?	Well, what's the reason for your call?
Darf ich fragen, um was es geht?	May I ask what it is concerned with?
Darf ich nach dem Grund Ihres Anrufs fragen?	May I ask the __________ of your call?

Time for a smile

A telephone cord only hangs freely with no kinks in television shows.

6. Getting through the waiting periods

Tut mir Leid, dass ich Sie habe warten lassen.	Sorry to have kept you waiting.
Tut mir Leid, aber ich bekomme keine Verbindung.	Sorry, but I can't get this number.
Frau Potter spricht gerade auf einer anderen Leitung.	Mrs Potter is ________ on ____________.
Tut mir sehr Leid, aber es wird gerade gesprochen.	I'm awfully sorry, but the line is ________________.

7. Leaving a message

Könnte ich eine Nachricht hinterlassen?	Could I leave a message, please?
Würden Sie John etwas von mir ausrichten?	Would you give John a message for me?
Würden Sie ihm bitte sagen, dass Bob Marley angerufen hat?	Would you please _________ him that Bob Marley ________?

8. Wrong number

Man hat Sie falsch verbunden.	You've got through to the wrong number.
Tut mir Leid, dies ist die falsche Nebenstelle.	Sorry, this is the wrong extension.
Entschuldigen Sie bitte, ich muss mich wohl verwählt haben.	I beg your pardon, I must have _________ the wrong number.

Time for a smile

The telephone will ring when you are having a shower. You will reach it just in time to hear the click of the caller hanging up.

9. Communication problems

Entschuldigen Sie bitte, aber das habe ich nicht mitbekommen.	I beg your pardon, but I missed that.
Könnten Sie das bitte wiederholen?	Could you repeat that, please?
Könnten Sie bitte langsamer sprechen?	Could you speak ______ , please?
Meinen Sie November oder September?	Do you __________ November or September?
Könnten Sie das buchstabieren?	Could you ______ that out for me?

TASK 4: Let's get it right

Which phrase is wrong?

1. May I assist you somehow other?
2. How can I help you?
3. Can I assist you in some way?

TASK 5: Typical German!

Please correct the grammar!

1. What can I for you do?
2. Who like you to speak?
3. I'd like to speak to your boss, if it goes.
4. I'm sorry, sir. I haven't quite caught your name.
5. Do I speak to Doors Inc.?
6. Are you spelling Brian with an 'i' or a 'y'?

The Psychologist's Corner

More and more business is done over the phone. If you want to be successful you must speak your partners' language, be on the wavelength of their brains. It's common knowledge today that our brain is divided in two parts. The left side processes facts and figures. The right side processes the way you present them: the images, the gestures and the tone of your voice that accompany your words. Good communicators reach the whole brain of their listeners, they keep both its sides busy.
Of course, you have to find out what type your business partner is. Is he or she the

- visual,
- auditive,
- or kinesthetic type?

Well, how do you find out? Simply by "watching" their language. What else could you do on the phone? So, just analyse the vocabulary they use.

1. The visual listeners

When they speak they use visual language like: *can you show me, can you give me an idea, bring some light into the dark, get a clear picture of, look at it from another angle* etc.
With them you should use visual language, imagery, metaphors and comparisons whenever possible. Tell them about the *size, shape* and *colours* of your product. Use concrete not abstract words and you will be on the same wavelength. Give them time to see the imagery of your language before their mind's eye.

2. The auditive listeners

They like music and a melodious voice that comes deep from the chest. Their language has few pictures to convey, they prefer words that describe sounds and noises. They will use phrases like: *that sounds interesting, I understand clearly what you mean, I want to say, an inner voice tells me that, there are rumours, may I summarise? I was speechless, I'm all ears ...* If you want to make them feel at home, don't use pictures, use auditive language: sounds and noises.

3. The kinesthetic or emotional listeners

They are neither visual nor auditive listeners. They are not people of many words, because it is easy for them to express feelings. They are often persons who enjoy working with their hands and feet: dancers, doctors, engineers. They prefer sports they can feel: swimming, hiking and they like spicy meals. They will use words that describe what you can touch with your hands or feel on your skin: *we can handle that, it feels like, I know how you feel about it, it smells a bit fishy, grasp, get in touch with, be under pressure, it goes under the skin, it was quite a shock for him.*

4.

Human beings are complex. Visual, auditive or kinesthetic types do not exist as ideal types. Most people are combinations of two or all three. So you if you have to address a large audience, appeal to all senses – to the eye of the visual type, to the ear of the auditive type and to the emotions of the kinesthetic type.

Let's take an example. How would you, as a clever car salesman, go about selling a car? Don't sell them a car – sell them colourful images, pleasant sounds and feelings. Make them hear the humming of a powerful engine, make them feel its vibration at their fingertips when they touch the mahogany steering wheel, the softness of the seats. And how it absorbs all the shocks of a bumpy road. Talk about the perfume of smooth leather, about the car's elegant, aerodynamic form and its sexy curves. And your audience will hang on your every word.

Time for a smile

It was two o'clock in the morning when Fred phoned Joe. The phone rang for half an hour before it was picked up and Joe's sleepy voice said, "Hello?" – "Sorry to get you out of bed at this time of night," said Fred. "That's all right," said Joe, "I had to get up anyway to answer the phone."

Ten commandments of telephone etiquette

Using the telephone professionally is more than knowing the correct phrases. Here are the ten commandments for operators, receptionists, secretaries and last but not least for bosses, some of whom have never been trained in how to use a phone and need these rules most.

1. Don't put anybody through on suspicion. Don't waste his or her time and money.
2. Make sure that he remembers numbers and names correctly. Ask if you should repeat the information you have given him.
3. Don't give the client an extension number without knowing if his or her contact is available.
4. Don't keep the caller waiting when you cannot put him through.
5. Don't bounce him back to the operator. Connect him personally.
6. Make sure that the relevant person is there and tell the caller what the call is about.
7. If it takes time to get through to the relevant person, don't park the caller; get back to him at intervals of 20 seconds and tell him why you had to make him wait.
8. Offer to call back, if you can't put the caller through.
9. Don't put the client through without apologising for having kept him waiting.
10. Thank him for his or her patience.

Time for a smile

Not knowing who you are talking to can be dangerous, as this phone story shows:
Tom and Tina had been married for twenty years without children. One day, the doctor told Tina that she was expecting a baby. Excitedly she rang up Tom at his office. "Tom, imagine, I am pregnant." – "That's great ..." exclaimed Tom. Then, after a long silence, Tom stuttered, "I beg your pardon, who is speaking?"

WORD AID

Adam; not know someone from ~	*jemanden überhaupt nicht kennen*
agenda	*Tagesordnung*
angle	*(Blick-)Winkel*
annoyed	*verärgert*
apologise	*sich entschuldigen*
apology	*Entschuldigung*
appeal to all senses	*alle Sinne ansprechen*
applicant	*Bewerber*
approach	*Methode, Verfahren*
assist	*helfen*
available	*erreichbar, verfügbar*
be all ears	*ganz Ohr sein*
bored	*gelangweilt*
bounce someone back to the operator	*zurück zur Vermittlung durchstellen*
brain	*Gehirn*
browse through	*durchblättern*
bumpy	*holprig*
caller	*Anrufer*
carry on	*weitermachen*
catch someone's name	*jemandes Namen verstehen*
chest	*Brust*
comparison	*Vergleich*
connect	*verbinden*
contact	*Kontaktperson*
convey	*übermitteln, mitteilen*
cut someone off	*jemanden aus der Leitung schmeißen*
depend on	*abhängen von*
do something on behalf of someone	*etwas für / im Auftrag von jemandem tun*
drop names	*Namen erwähnen*
effort	*Anstrengung, Mühe*
extension	*Nebenstelle, Durchwahl*
grasp	*erfassen*

hang up	*(den Hörer) auflegen*
hiking	*Wandern*
hum	*summen*
human resources department	*Personalabteilung*
judge someone	*jemanden beurteilen*
kinesthetic (kinetic&esthetic)	*etwa: bewegungsästhetisch*
kink	*Schleife; verknäulen, verknoten*
on suspicion	*auf Verdacht*
operator	*Vermittlung*
patience	*Geduld*
prefer	*vorziehen*
pressure	*Druck*
put someone through to	*jemanden verbinden mit*
receive the information	*die Information erhalten*
receiver	*Telefonhörer*
reception	*Empfang*
recipient	*Empfänger*
relevant person	*die betreffende Person*
reward	*Belohnung*
rumour	*Gerücht*
sales supervisor	*Verkaufsleiter*
shape	*Form, Gestalt*
size	*Größe*
smell fishy	*faul sein; nicht stimmen*
smells a bit fishy	*das riecht verdächtig (übertragen)*
smooth	*glatt*
softness	*Weichheit*
sound	*klingen*
spell	*buchstabieren*
spicy (hot)	*gewürzt*
spicy meals	*gewürzte Speisen*
successful	*erfolgreich*
touch	*Berührung, Gefühl, Tastsinn*
voice	*Stimme*
waste	*verschwenden*
wavelength	*Wellenlänge*

Module 9

WRITING FOR EFFECT (2)

MEMOS AND E-MAILS

Most companies probably have problems with their internal communication. An explosion of note-passing and e-mailing has taken place which has caused confusion. Members of staff waste a lot of time dealing with private or incomprehensible messages. Hardman is fed up with it all!

We focus on

- when and why write a memo
- form and structure of memos
- the style of a memo

Tidying up at Busoom

"And I'm fed up with it," Hardman thundered. "Employees pass scruffy little sheets of paper to each other with half-written illegible messages on them, there are numerous telephone calls about God and the world, but rarely about the business, and there are streams of e-mails which block up all the real work-processes."
He called together an extraordinary meeting of the top management circle. This should have included Seaweed (**S**), Ramsch, Dr Geisel, and Hardman's (**H**) personal assistant, Mrs Velvet (**V**). Unfortunately Mr Ramsch and Dr Geisel could not be there. They were on holiday.

H: Why wasn't I informed about the problems with our revolver? I seem to be the last one to be told about important things. Lack of communication and that means lack of operational excellence.

S: There's certainly some misunderstanding going on. You were sent an internal memo.

H: Internal memo? I wouldn't even know one if I saw one. Have we got a standardised format? Look here! This is an example of what I get on my desk every day. (*Mr Hardman had made a transparency of the following memo*)

> *Info for*
> *Mr Hardman.*
> *Please note. Purchasing manager of Oldie wants*
> *quick appointment about doors.*
> *(illegible signature)*

H: It took me nearly an hour to find out who had taken this message and what it was all about.

V: I'm not surprised. Everyone just leaves messages as they feel like it. You've got to be happy to get the message at all.
(*Hardman smashed his folder down on the conference table. His papers flew in all directions.*)

H: That's just it. No communication. No standards! Where's the operational excellence? Look, today, I want us to set standards. At least what should be included, and how it should be designed. We're one company. We need standard forms of internal communication.

S: Well, we are all individuals, and ...

H: (*interrupting loudly*) Our company, our collective is greater than any individual.

S: Right, if you say so.

H: I do. Now look at the OHP. I want to fix standards on what a memo should look like. Here it is:

> **MEMO Busoom Internal**
> **Purpose:** Presenting our revolver
> **From:** Seaweed, Director of admin.
> **To:** Hardman, CEO, Busoom Ltd.
> **Date:** 6/8/2001
> **Subject:** Problems with power revolver
> **Copy list:** First Line Management
>
> Presentation of power revolver was a disaster. Purchasing manager of Oldie wants quick appointment to discuss complaints about power revolver.
>
> **Action to be taken:**
> Meeting of all concerned. Seminar on presentation.
> *Seaweed*

H: You'll all get the standardised form; it'll be on your laptops. Make sure all your staff get it. It is obligatory. They must follow this format.

S: I don't know how that'll go down.

H: It will go down or they'll go down. Now look what's important: date, and as far as I'm concerned also the time when sent, the subject, what's it all about, the contents, background, etc., and a clear signature.

S: There'll be reactions to all this. It's extra work.

H: The employees are paid to work. This company is not a democracy. It's a company and it has to work hyper-efficiently, or people will simply lose their jobs. Now, the next point is the e-mail. It should be an aid to communication, but I feel it costs us three hundred percent too much lost time. And you won't believe it but I have checked the e-mail situation and fifty percent of e-mails received were private, and not company business. You could've knocked me down with a feather when I saw that. Is this a business or a playground for pleasure seekers?

V: Mr Hardman, I think you're exaggerating a bit.

H: Probably, but there's more than a grain of truth in all that. Now about all these e-mails. I'm going to have a list of rules. I want meaningful titles at the top of the mail and, so everyone knows what's it about, it should be as short as possible, it should only deal with our business. Don't attach extra files if you're mailing a lot of people. And no rude language or insults. If I get to know about any of that the sender will be on the carpet. And another thing ... *(fade out)*

WORKING with the language

TASK 1: Business phrases to remember

den Betrieb aufhalten	block _____ work-_________
Da liegt ein Missverständnis vor.	There's some misunderstanding _________ _____.
Da ist ein Körnchen Wahrheit dran.	There's a ______ of ______ in it.
jemandem etwas ausrichten	_______ a message ____ someone
Die Botschaft wurde gut aufgenommen.	The message went _____ _____.
Anforderungen stellen	_____ standards
zusammengestaucht werden	be _____ the _____

The Analyst's Corner

TASK 2: Getting the message

1. What is it that makes Hardman very angry regarding communication?
2. What is a simple solution that Hardman would like to introduce as soon as possible?
3. Can you explain what Mr Hardman wanted to communicate with these phrases?
   - **A.** You could've knocked me down with a feather.
   - **B.** They'll go down.

TASK 3: What do you know about internal memoranda?

Take a stand	Yes	No
1. Should you prepare a memorandum at the end of discussions, conversations or telephone calls?		
2. Mr Rum messed up a presentation. Do you write him a memo?		
3. Do you keep the list of recipients as short as possible?		
4. If you want to keep a memo secret do you mark it "To whom it may concern"?		
5. If the memo is top secret, do you mark it "Confidential"?		
6. Memos should only be read in the office. Don't take them home.		
7. Is this sentence memo style? *Consideration should be given to the possibility of carrying plan B into effect as suggested by the consultants.* Why (not)?		
8. If your memo is more than two pages do you add a contents list?		
9. Should you leave generous space between paragraphs and at the bottom of the page?		
10. Do you leave a wide margin on both sides of the page?		

TASK 4: The perfect memo

Even if you didn't fail our quiz, you'll find sound advice here. And to practise your English translate the German in brackets. Here's some help for you. Careful, you might have to change the word form a little.

suggest	prove	immediate
twice	waste	appoint
supplier	emphasize	violation

When is a memorandum justified?

Some managers use memoranda as a dumping ground for any odd ideas that come to their mind whether important and of interest to their colleagues, or not. They (*1. verstoßen gegen*) a cardinal rule of business etiquette: Don't (*2. verschwenden*) your colleague's time! Think (*3. zweimal*) before you write a memorandum. If you need (*4. sofortiges*) feedback, make a telephone call or arrange an (*5. Termin*).

Write a memo only if ...

- you need the memo for personal use: as (*6. Beweis*) that you have taken action, as the record of a decision or a conversation which might be of reference value one day.
- you want to express or (*7. betonen*) your views.
- you want to put forward (*8. Vorschläge*).
- you want to (*9. geben, liefern*) information that would otherwise take too long to reach all who need it.

Time for a smile (Does this one ring a bell?)

Executive overheard talking to a friend: "My wife tells me I don't display enough passion. Imagine! I have a good mind to send her a memo."

TASK 5: The structure of the memo

You'll find more advice for perfecting your memos. And to practise your English (see Task 4).

subject	overview	limit
contain	purpose	addressee
head	margin	remedy

Since memos are often read in a car or on a train they should be catchy. A good memo is only memorable if it has a clear structure. This skeleton memo is about training the staff to present the products more efficiently.

Date: July 10, 2002

Main title: **Training needs**

State the (*1. Zweck*). Say in one, two or three words what the memo is about.

(*2. Thema*): **Improving product presentations**

From: Don't waste your colleague's time. The list of (*3. Adressaten*), the copy list, should be (*4. beschränkt*).

To: to those who need the information

(*5. **Inhalt***): If your memo has more than two pages give the reader an (*6. Überblick*). State what he will find on each page.

Page 1: Background: Embarrassing incidents

Page 2: Suggestion: How to (*7. abhelfen*) shortcomings

Page 3: Seminar providers and costs

(*8. Titel*): A contents list only makes sense if your memo has a clear structure. Each paragraph should have a (*8. Überschrift*).

Margin and spaces: Leave wide (*9. Ränder*) on both sides of the page and generous space between paragraphs and at the bottom of the page to allow readers to make notes.

Form and Style: How to write a memo

The cardinal rule of business etiquette: don't waste your colleagues' time.

Recipient: the more senior the recipient, the shorter the memo.
Length: be brief: short memos get read; long memos don't. The length should be appropriate to subject matter and recipient – as short as possible, as long as necessary.
Paragraphs: seven lines plus / minus two
Sentences: short ones are understood, long ones aren't.
Churchill wrote in a memo to his government departments: Let us have an end of phrases like these: *It is also of importance to bear in mind the following consideration ... or Consideration should be given to the possibility of carrying into effect ...* Most of these woolly phrases ... can be left out altogether or replaced by a single word.
Words: never use a long word where a short one will do, never use a scientific or foreign word when there is an everyday English one (George Orwell). If the matter is complex or abstract, use an example.
In a nutshell: Justify every word, sentence, paragraph and when in doubt, leave out.

TASK 6: How would Churchill have said it?

1. *It is also of importance to bear in mind the following consideration ...* (Use four to five words instead of 13)
2. *Consideration should be given to the possibility of carrying into effect plan B.* (Use not more than six to eight words)

Office Arithmetic

Smart boss + smart employee = profit
Smart boss + dumb employee = production
Dumb boss + dumb employee = overtime

The KISS principle

Keep it short, simple, stupid. Written messages should be understood by your most unintelligent employee. A message can be short, simple but not clear – as this anecdote about J. Edgar Hoover, former director of the FBI, shows:
A young man was appointed head of FBI's stores and stationery. New brooms sweep clean. Eager to make a good impression he tried to cut down costs. Among other attempts to save money he reduced the size of the margins of the memo paper. When the new memo pads landed on Hoover's desk he found that the margins on both sides of the paper were not wide enough. So he wrote across the sheet in big letters:

WATCH THE BORDERS

His message was short, simple but not clear. His secretary misinterpreted the note and so, for the next couple of weeks, it became extremely difficult to enter the USA by car either from Canada or Mexico.

WORD AID

addressee	*Adressat*
aid	*Hilfe*
appointment	*Termin, Verabredung*
at least	*wenigstens*
carpet; be on the ~	*zusammengestaucht werden*
catchy	*auffällig, ins Auge fallend*
complaint	*Reklamation, Beschwerde*
concern	*betreffen; Sorge*
concerned	*Betroffene(r)*
confidential	*vertraulich*

consideration	*Erwägung, Betrachtung*
content(s)	*Inhalt*
design	*gestalten*
disaster	*Katastrophe*
display passion	*Leidenschaft an den Tag legen*
dumb	*dumm*
dumping ground	*Müllhalde*
embarrassing incidents	*peinliche Vorfälle*
emphasize	*betonen, hervorheben*
exaggerate	*übertreiben*
excellence	*Vortrefflichkeit, vorzügliche Leistung*
fed; be ~ up with	*die Nase voll haben von*
file	*Datei, Akte*
folder	*Aktenordner*
generous	*großzügig*
go down	*ankommen, aufgenommen werden*
grain of truth	*Körnchen Wahrheit*
heading	*Titel, Überschrift*
illegible	*unleserlich*
include	*mit einschließen, beinhalten*
incomprehensible	*unverständlich*
insult	*Beleidigung*
internal	*intern*
lack of	*Mangel an*
leave a message	*eine Nachricht hinterlassen*
margin	*Rand*
mess something up	*vermasseln, verpfuschen*
nutshell; in a~	*Nussschale; kurz gesagt*
obligatory	*verpflichtend*
operational excellence	*optimale Leistung am Arbeitsplatz*
overtime	*Überstunden*
proof	*Beweis*
prove	*beweisen*
purpose	*Zweck*
put forward plans	*Pläne vorlegen*

recipient	*Empfänger*
reference	*Beleg, Bezug*
remedy	*Heilmittel; abhelfen, abstellen*
rude	*unhöflich, grob*
scruffy	*schmuddelig, dreckig*
set standards	*Anforderungen stellen*
sick	*krank*
simultaneous	*gleichzeitig*
smash something down	*etwas hinknallen*
sound advice	*vernünftiger Rat*
space	*Abstand, Raum*
subject	*Thema*
suggest	*empfehlen*
supplier	*Lieferant*
supply	*liefern*
take a message for someone	*jemandem etwas ausrichten*
take action	*etwas unternehmen, aktiv werden*
tidy up	*aufräumen, säubern*
transparency	*Overheadfolie*
value	*Wert*
violate a rule	*gegen eine Regel verstoßen*
waste	*verschwenden*
woolly phrases	*verschwommene Sätze*
work-processes	*Arbeitsabläufe*

10 Module

COACHING AND COUNSELLING

TIDYING UP AT BUSOOM

We've dealt with these two topics in one chapter as we feel they are closely related. Of course, we know that coaching is more one-to-one training of a specific skill or generally presenting information to an individual or group. Counselling focusses more on personal problems and perhaps involves more listening. Let's see how Busoom gets on.

We focus on

- improving performance: coaching
- helping employees with problems: counselling
- useful phrases for counsellors

Smoothing over the cracks

At Busoom, as at any other company, problems arise between members of staff. Seaweed is beginning to get reports from various departments of stress and tension among some employees. He decides to intervene personally by giving advice, by helping to train the employees a little. In other words he wants to implement an intelligent mixture of coaching and counselling.

Hardman (**H**) and Seaweed (**S**)

H: So you are going to advise them yourself. I don't know if it'll work. You know the coach has to encourage staff, give them tips on how to improve performance, get more know-how, set goals, etc.

S: I know, I know, and counselling is discussing problems that an employee has at work or privately. But we're so short of time and I feel the two things fit together.

H: Okay. Do as you see fit, but make it work!

So off went Seaweed and arranged a one-to-one meeting with Mr Loud from Information Technology.

L: So, what's this interview all about? I guess some of my colleagues have complained about me. Well, they just don't understand anything[1].

S: No, no, Mr Loud, nobody has said anything. I'll be talking to several people during the next few days. I'm here to help to move things forward. First of all I'd like to ask you about your work. How do you feel things are going?

L: Well, since you ask, I feel I'm being overloaded with work. The phone rings all the time. I can't seem to manage.

S: And then I suppose you start getting angry, with your colleagues at the office?[2]

L: It happens. I feel I should be earning more for all this work and stress.

S: I'm sure we all feel we should be earning more. I certainly do. But there are other ways we can help. From what you've been telling me you could use some help with your time planning. Would you be willing to attend a seminar in Personal Time Management? It's over a weekend[3].

---

1 The numbers refer to the questions in the Analyst's Corner and to the answers in the Key.

L: I hadn't thought about that. Perhaps it's a good idea. Why not? I'll give it a try.

S: Now, let's try[4] to solve the phone-call issue. First of all I'd like to tell you that it's a difficulty we all have. It's not just you suffering. We're all in the same boat. So don't worry! If you agree, I'd suggest the following strategy. We separate the calls, most of them are internal, into absolute priorities, you deal with them on the spot. All others should be told that they will be phoned back within a certain period of time, say by the end of the day. And we fix a system that you pass the info about the call on to a given colleague. Then we are sure that someone will get back to the internal customer.

L: Sounds okay to me.

S: Great![5] By the way I heard on the grapevine that you've been having some personal problems.

L: Well, of course it's nothing to do with the company ...

S: If we can help in any way.

L: It's my wife. She's been taken ill, and it's a problem with the children and their times.

S: Why don't we sit together with Mrs Velvet and work out a temporary schedule that gives you some help? You know ... (*fade out*)

The Analyst's Corner

TASK 1: Did you get the message?

1. How should Seaweed react after this defensive sort of statement from Mr Loud?
2. "And then I suppose ..." What does Seaweed want to achieve with this approach?
3. In which ways does Seaweed communicate his suggestions? How does he avoid or deal with the question of more money for Loud?
4. Which clever tactics does Seaweed use to show Loud that he is not alone with his problems?
5. Can you comment on Seaweed's sentence beginning: "Great, ..."?

WORKING with the language

TASK 2: Business phrases to remember

Fill in the missing words

Spannungen mit Angestellten	________ with employees
persönlich einschreiten	________ personally
Ziele stecken	________ goals
Er schafft es nicht, es ist ihm nicht möglich.	He can't ________.
Berichte aus den Abteilungen	________ from the ________

TASK 3: Bits and pieces

etwas gerüchteweise hören	hear something ________ the grapevine
Tun Sie, was Sie für richtig halten.	Do ____ you see fit.
sich damit sofort befassen	deal ____ it ____ the spot
Tipps, wie man die Leistung verbessert	tips __ ____ to improve performance

TASK 4: Phrases for counsellors – personal problems

1. How to start the conversation

Es geht mich vielleicht nichts an, aber ...	Perhaps it's not my ________, but ...
Ich sollte mich vielleicht nicht einmischen, aber ...	Perhaps I should keep my ________ out of it, but ...
Halten Sie mich bitte nicht für neugierig, aber ...	Don't think I'm sticking my ________ in, but ...
Halten Sie mich bitte nicht für neugierig, aber ...	Don't think I'm being ________, but ...

2. Expressing sympathy

Ich habe das Gefühl, Sie bedrückt etwas.	I think you've got something on your _________ .
Sie sind mit Ihren Gedanken in der letzten Zeit ganz woanders.	In the last few days you've had your ________ on something else.
Haben Sie Sorgen?	Are you ______ about something?
Sie machen ein Gesicht wie drei Tage Regenwetter.	You're really going around with a long _________ .

3. Creating an atmosphere of confidence

Sie können ganz offen sprechen.	You can speak _________ .
Wir sollten uns einmal unter vier Augen unterhalten?	We should talk about it ________ .
Es bleibt alles unter uns.	We'll keep it to ________.
unter vier Augen	just _________ you and me
Wo drückt der Schuh?	What's _________ you?
Wir sind doch keine Unmenschen.	We aren't _________ , you know.

4. Offering a shoulder to cry on

Nehmen Sie mein Taschentuch.	Use my _________ .
Ich kann mir vorstellen, wie Ihnen zumute ist.	I can _________ how you feel.
Das kann jedem von uns passieren.	It can _________ to anyone. These things can ________ .
Nichts wird so heiß gegessen, wie es gekocht wird.	It's never ____ bad ____ it seems.
Lassen Sie sich ruhig Zeit.	_________ your time.

5. Offering support

Kann ich irgendetwas für Sie tun?	Is there anything ______ I can do?
Kann ich Ihnen irgendwie helfen?	Can I ________ help somehow?
Gibt es etwas, das ich tun könnte?	Can I help in _________ way?

6. Looking for a solution

Es gibt immer einen Ausweg.	There's always some ________ .
Wir werden gemeinsam eine Lösung finden.	We'll find a ________ together.
Haben Sie schon einmal mit dem Betriebsrat gesprochen?	Have you already spoken to the ________ ?
Möchten Sie, dass ich mit ... spreche?	Do you ________ to speak to ...?
Lassen Sie das unseren Justiziar machen, dazu ist er da.	Our ________ should do it. That's what he's paid for.
Nach Regen kommt Sonnenschein.	Every ________ has a silver lining.
Kommt Zeit, kommt Rat.	Time will ________ .

The Communicator's Corner

TASK 5: Test yourself – How good a coach are you?

Take a stand	Yes	No
1. You should meet staff regularly at least monthly.		
2. These meetings should always be informal.		
3. Coaching means annual appraisals and performance reviews.		
4. Do you give them the performance review a week beforehand?		
5. You should avoid any confrontation.		
6. The main aim of coaching is to improve the working climate.		
7. The main aim of coaching is to improve performance.		
8. You shouldn't hesitate to discuss any weaknesses of an employee.		
9. Coaching should be formal. Prepare an agenda.		
10. Don't coach without the consent of the employee.		

What coaching is all about

1. Why coaching is necessary

Coaching is one way to achieve higher standards by discussing the weaknesses and the strengths of the employees. You should offer training, help them to gain more confidence, encourage them to take more responsibilities and to define personal targets.

2. Setting the stage

Coaching can be done informally at the office or on neutral territory. A formal one-to-one meeting in the company should be held every two weeks or at least once a month. You should invite them a couple of days in advance for this meeting. Give them a written review of their performance and the agenda. They need the time to prepare their response.

3. Structure the meeting

In case of a formal meeting, come to the point quickly, keep to the agenda, sum up the results and make sure he or she agrees with the summary.

4. Striking the right tone

This is not the time for emotions. The conversation should be perfectly honest and rational but always polite. Listen patiently to what they have to say. Confrontation is sometimes unavoidable, even necessary, but the employee should be able to leave with his dignity intact.

Time for a smile

An office manager said to the new cleaning woman, "I hope you don't mind me saying this, but there's still a lot of dust on this desk! It looks as if it hasn't been dusted for months!"
"How should I know?" replied the cleaning woman. "I've only been working here for two weeks."

TASK 6: Test yourself: How good a counsellor are you?

Take a stand	Yes	No
1. Your secretary has a problem. You discuss it with her.		
2. If the problem affects her job you inform your boss.		
3. You give her sound advice; you appeal to reason and logic.		
4. If you want to influence her, appeal to emotions.		
5. It is your job to suggest a solution to her problem.		
6. You help her to help herself. Let her find a solution.		
7. Offer several ways to reach the goal. Leave her the choice.		
8. Help to establish a plan for reaching the goal.		
9. Observe over a period of time how she is coping.		
10. Set a deadline by which you expect her to have solved the problem.		

What not to say as a coach

My dear Dobson, you aren't the sharpest knife in our drawer.

❖

According to the test you've got a room temperature IQ.

❖

You'd be out of your depth in a parking lot puddle.

What counselling is all about

Developing the skills to help and support people is important. Let's take an example. You spot a change in the behaviour of your secretary which signals that all is not well. Next you realize that her performance isn't what it used to be. Spotting the change is fairly easy, however, it is not so easy to find out what has caused the change. What do you do?

Analyse the situation

- First, it is your right to find out why she is not doing her job properly. It is not that you are nosy, it is simply that her failure to perform to standard is your concern.

- Second, it is your duty to help her to work out a solution to her troubles. And unless you know the cause, you cannot help her. You need to discuss this to see what can be done to improve her situation.
- Third, and above all, you need to keep the content of your discussions confidential, otherwise no one will ever trust you with personal matters again.

Help her to find her own solution

- Before you suggest counselling to a member of the staff, make sure that they agree they have a problem that needs help.
- The first step is to her talk, to listen, to help her clarify the situation and get to the root of the problem.
- The second step is the key to counselling. Prompt her to come up with useful suggestions as to how she can help herself. Don't try to solve the problem for her, don't suggest solutions.
- Make things easier for her, perhaps altering the hours for a while to alleviate domestic difficulties.
- Whatever help is given you need to check how the she is coping.

Time for smile

"Dobson," said the boss one morning, "I just don't know how we are going to get along without you – but starting Monday, we're going to try."

The Psychologist's Corner

The choice is theirs

The best approach is to let the person know ahead of time that he has the final say on what he ultimately does.

Don't be a know-all

Nobody wants to hear advice from a "know-all." One of the very best ways of offering advice is to let the person know that you don't believe you have all the answers.

Appeal to emotions

Counselling is influencing and advising. If you want to counsel a person you need to appeal to a person's emotions. Ninety percent of the decisions we make are based on emotion. We then use logic to justify our actions. If you appeal to someone on a strictly logical basis, you'll have little chance of persuading him.

Don't push, pull

Try to remind someone that it was he who first had the idea or put you in the right direction. Let him know, too, that this new way of thinking is really consistent with who he is. Here Seaweed failed.

Show the way

When you want them to follow your advice give them a map for getting there. Offer a specific plan, a clear-cut course of action for moving forward. It is essential that we understand the direction and the method for proceeding. It makes us feel comfortable and secure knowing that the path is clearly laid out. Seaweed got it right.

Deviations from the right way are dangerous

Add to this how your ideas prevent negative or unpleasant consequences. This is more effective than explaining what someone will gain. If you add to this how your idea will prevent negative or unpleasant consequences, you will be infinitely more successful in your attempt to influence.

Enthusiasm is contagious

The more excited and passionate you are about what you're saying, the more excited your listener will become about it. If you are not excited about the idea, he will not be excited about it either.

WORD AID

achieve something	*etwas erreichen, leisten*
advice	*Rat*
advise	*raten*
affect	*beeinträchtigen, beeinflussen*
agenda	*Tagesordnung*
alleviate	*lindern, mildern*
annual	*jährlich*
appeal to emotions	*Gefühle ansprechen*
appraisal	*Beurteilung*
approach	*Methode, Strategie*
arise, arose, arisen; problems ~	*Probleme entstehen*
avoid	*vermeiden*
behaviour	*Verhalten*
bother	*beunruhigen, quälen, bedrücken*
choice	*Wahl*
coaching	*Unterweisung, Anleitung*
concern	*Angelegenheit, Interesse, Sorge*
confidence	*Selbstvertrauen, Zuversicht*
consent	*Zustimmung*
consistent	*übereinstimmend, vereinbar, konstant*
contagious	*ansteckend*
cope with	*fertig werden mit*
counselling	*Beratung*
cracks; smooth over ~	*Sprünge, Risse kitten*
deadline	*Fristablauf, Stichtag*
deal with a topic	*ein Thema behandeln*
defensive	*abwehrend, schützend*
deviation	*Abweichung*
dignity	*Würde*
domestic difficulties	*häusliche Probleme*
drawer	*Schublade*
dust	*Staub; staubwischen*

duty	*Pflicht*
earn more	*mehr Geld verdienen*
essential	*wichtig, wesentlich*
failure	*Versagen*
given; a ~ colleague	*ein bestimmter Kollege*
goal	*Ziel*
grapevine; hear on the ~	*etwas gerüchteweise hören*
honest	*ehrlich*
implement	*aus-, durchführen*
interfere	*sich einmischen*
involve	*betreffen, angehen*
legal advisor	*Justiziar*
nosy	*neugierig*
outset, from the ~	*von Anfang an*
parking lot	*Parkplatz*
performance	*Leistung*
point; come to the ~	*zur Sache kommen*
prompt someone to do something	*jemanden veranlassen, etwas zu tun*
properly	*ordentlich*
puddle	*Pfütze*
related; closely ~	*nahe verwandt*
response	*Antwort, Reaktion*
review	*Kritik, Bericht*
root of the problem	*Wurzel des Problems*
see fit	*für richtig halten*
smooth over	*glätten*
spot	*ausmachen, erkennen, erblicken*
spot; on the ~	*sofort*
strength	*Stärke*
suggestion	*Vorschlag, Anregung*
suppose	*annehmen, vermuten*
target	*Ziel*
tension	*Spannung*
unavoidable	*unvermeidlich*
works council	*Betriebsrat*
worried	*besorgt*

11 Module

COMMUNICATING YOUR IMAGE

GO TELL IT ON THE MOUNTAINS ...

Individuals communicate (or perhaps they don't). Companies also communicate. Communication takes place between companies, between manufacturers and their customers, though on a different level and on a larger scale. No matter what channel or media you choose, one part of your message is the company's image. It is omnipresent and should be crystal clear, uniform, homogeneous and standardized.

We focus on

- phrases to present the company
- the form of press releases
- other means of getting your image across

Go tell it on the mountains ...

In the past six months Hardman has been taking a hard man's look at some processes and standards at Busoom. One of his favourites is "company image" and "communicating with the customer". He is talking to Dr Geisel about it (but not with much success).
"What's your opinion about our stationery and logo then?" Hardman put his question very directly.
"It's okay, I guess."
"Is 'okay' the most motivating word you can find?"
"Of course not, of course not. It's fine, I wanted to say."
Hardman was unhappy. "There's a big difference between 'okay' and 'fine', isn't there?"
Dr Geisel jerked his head as if avoiding a heavyweight boxing punch. "Of course, of course."

To cut a long story short the discussion was not very satisfactory. Hardman booked himself a three-day seminar on "A new view on communication" and "Let your customers really know". A week later he handed his newly acquired wisdom down to his directors and first-line managers. It went something like this:

(*fade in*) ... so did you, my dear colleagues, ever have the feeling that our business stationery looks very ordinary? Does it show, does it communicate what Busoom is really about? No, it doesn't. Our logo is our advertisement. It mirrors the company's image. It's got to exactly show what we do and how we're different from the rest. And when we have it, it should always appear in our standard design.
At present, I'm looking into our corporate communication and I'm dissatisfied. Everybody writes what he feels like. I want to see our corporate identity on the following:

letterheads	invoices	compliment slips
envelopes	business cards	stickers
order forms	leaflets	brochures
catalogues	posters	bulletins
newsletters	packaging signs	displays etc.

As I hope you know, PR means getting Busoom into the press, local TV or any other media, but giving it a positive image. Positive stories about Busoom. And somehow we have not been getting into the public eye. The trick is, my dear fellows, when you send something to the editor, you have to make sure you catch his eye. Will your article interest his readers? I'll give you an example of what will certainly not catch the editor's attention. Recently we sent the following prize item to a trade journal:
"Busoom has developed a new door!" Well, gentlemen, that's absolutely marvellous. Of what interest is that? It's our job to develop doors. So what's new? What's fascinating? You have to be creative: You have to list up, and that in the first paragraph, things of real interest, anything that is completely unique to Busoom. And keep it short. And then not too much detail. Include any good quotes or references. Now off with you, go tell it on the mountains that Busoom has fantastic doors.

WORKING with the language

TASK 1: How good is your memory?

Aufmerksamkeit der Öffentlichkeit erregen	___________ into the public eye
jemanden auf sich aufmerksam machen	___________ someone's attention
Ergebnisse beobachten / verfolgen	___________ results
zurück zu unserem Thema	___________ to our ___________
den Absatz fördern	___________ sales

Words of Wisdom

The most truthful part of a newspaper is the advertisements.
Thomas Jefferson

TASK 2: Presenting the company

Words and phrases to present your company

beschäftigen	employ
schnell wachsen	expand rapidly
gründen	found
Marktführer	market leader
mittelgroß	medium-sized
Tätigkeit	operations
Einzelhandelsgeschäft	retail outlet
Tochtergesellschaft	subsidiary

Fit in the words from the box. Be careful to use the correct form.

1. We are a ________ - ________ company.
2. Our company ________ ________ 25 years ago.
3. Our company ________ ________ rapidly.
4. We have ______________ located in five cities.
5. The company ______________ over two hundred people.
6. We supply doors through ________ ________ all over Britain.
7. Our principal ______________ are in revolving and sliding doors.
8. We pride ourselves in being the ________ ________ .

TASK 3: First steps towards a mission statement

diversify	requirement	breakthrough
supplier	sector	grow
user	innovate	convey
range	needs	attention

The words in the box will help you translate the German in the following text.
Mind the form of the words!

Busoom's – the communicator between people and places

Busoom is one of Europe's leading (*1. Lieferant*) of doors. The company (*2. beschäftigt*) over 200 people and has (*3. Tochtergesellschaft*) located in five cities. Since its (*4. Gründung*) in 1975 the company (*5. wachsen*) rapidly to meet the (*6. Nachfrage*) of both young and old. The company has always recognised the (*7. Anforderungen*) of changing market (*8. Bedürfnisse*) and (*9. diversifizieren*) and (*10. erneuern*) its product (*11. Reihe*) in time. The (*12. Durchbruch*) came with the microchip. The computerised revolving and sliding doors have even caught the (*13. Aufmerksamkeit*) of various institutions at home and abroad. Why?
The Busoom door is more than a door, it is a means of communication in the broader sense of the phrase. Not only does it link rooms and places, it actually communicates with its (*14. Benutzern*). It recognises them, greets them, speaks their names and can (*15. übermitteln*) messages.

TASK 4: Communication quiz about 'Imaging'

1. What's the name given to exhibitions of products taking place annually and intended for potential customers?
2. Famous companies give money to support products in sport. What is this system of communication called?
3. We place information in the press, items of interest about our company, the products, etc. What do we call this work?
4. A type of direct mailing where advertising material is placed directly through the letter box.
5. The system where thousands of leaflets are sent out to potential customers as mass coverage.
6. What is the sales tactic called where the sales staff visit potential customers to explain product info to them?

True or False?

7. The most effective advertising is positive word-of-mouth advertising.
8. Press releases are more expensive than advertising in the media.
9. Press releases – the quantity is more important than the quality.

The Communicator's Corner

1. The mission statement

A company that is new on the market should introduce itself to the world of business. A mission statement is one of the opportunities of presenting your company. If you plan to create a website it could be part of it.
The mission statement on the website is special. It should be short and compact like a slogan. It is a commitment for the future and could be formulated as follows:

It is our goal to develop a close relationship with ...
It is our target to protect the environment, etc.

Using this style the mission statement could do the following:

1. introduce the company
2. present your product range
3. present the staff
4. give testimonials from customers
5. name your suppliers
6. bring all these loose ends together

2. The press release

The main point of a press release is to spread news about your product or service. There are hundreds of trade journals and specialist magazines whose role it is to inform readers about new products. The question is whether or not the editor thinks the subject will be of interest to his readership. It is therefore of major importance that your release is presented in the best possible light. Make it one page only.

1. Step: Say what is new or special in the first paragraph.
2. Step: Describe the benefits for everyone who buys from you or works with you.
3. Step: When and how can they get the product? How can they reach you?

Let's take an example. Hardman was very proud of his release. Here's how he 'sold' the new Communicative Busoom Revolver Deluxe-I (*I* is short for *intelligent*) to the press.

The hottest innovation of this year

Intelligent Busoom revolvers revolutionize the door market

Busoom has developed a new revolving door. The conventional door has served only two rather unintelligent purposes:

1. to let you in and out or
2. to keep you in or out

The new Communicative Busoom Revolver Deluxe-I can do a lot more. Just to mention three of its many intelligent features:

1. Busoom Revolver Deluxe-I greets the visitor with a friendly "Welcome to our company. Your success is our pursuit."
2. When customers leave the company Busoom Revolver Deluxe-I will again whisper "Your success is our pursuit" plus some friendly words of farewell into their ears. You can choose between hundreds of different varieties, from "We wish you a good day", "We hope to see you again soon", "Take care", to "God bless you!" or "Jesus loves you" (for church doors).
3. A video monitor identifies important customers and you can customise the words of welcome or farewell accordingly: "Good afternoon, Mr Dwarf. What a pleasure to see you again" or "Good-bye, Mr McNab. Please remember us to Mrs McNab."

Busoom Revolver Deluxe-I, the first of its kind, comes complete with cameras, speakers plus software. It retails at $1485 and will help you to create a lasting relationship between you and your customers. We pride ourselves in being able to adapt the revolver to individual needs, for example

- the Busoom Revolver Deluxe-Mu for export-orientated customers is a musical door that features 98 national anthems;
- the Busoom Revolver Deluxe-Di for zoos, hotels and swimming pools imperceptibly disinfects visitors' shoes and clothes against foot and mouth disease, mad cow disease and other viruses.

For presentations please contact
H. Hardman, CEO; Busoom Ltd.
Tel.: 04231 99 66 44 00; Fax: 04231 99 66 44 11

WORD AID

accordingly	*entsprechend*
appear	*erscheinen*
avoid	*vermeiden*
benefits	*Vorteile, Nutzen*
bless	*segnen*
bloom	*Blüte*
business stationery	*Firmenbriefpapier*
by word of mouth	*mündlich*
compliment slip	*Grußkarte*
conventional	*herkömmlich*
convey	*mitteilen, vermitteln*
corporate communication	*firmenspezifische Kommunikation*
corporate identity	*Firmencharakter*
customise	*maßschneidern*
directory	*(Telefon-)Verzeichnis*
face-to-face contact	*persönliches Gespräch*
feature	*Eigenschaft*
first-line managers	*Direktionsebene*
foot and mouth disease	*Maul- und Klauenseuche*
imperceptibly	*unmerklich*
intended for	*vorgesehen, bestimmt für*
invoice	*Rechnung*
item of interest	*etwas von Interesse*
jerk one's head	*mit dem Kopf zucken*
leaflet	*Faltblatt, Werbezettel*
letterhead	*Briefkopf*
mission	*Sendung, Berufung, Aufgabe*
mission statement	*gestecktes Ziel*
national anthem	*Nationalhymne*
omnipresent	*allgegenwärtig*
order form	*Bestellformular*
petal	*Blütenblatt*

press release	*Pressemitteilung*
pride oneself on	*stolz sein auf*
principal	*haupt-, hauptsächlich*
processes	*Geschäftsabläufe*
public eye; get into the ~~	*das Interesse der Öffentlichkeit erregen*
purpose	*Ziel, Zweck*
pursuit	*Streben*
quote	*Zitat*
recently	*küzlich; in letzter Zeit*
reference	*Referenz; Empfehlung, Bezug*
remember us to ...	*grüßen Sie ... von uns*
rep (representative)	*Vertreter*
retail at	*der Ladenpreis beträgt*
sturdy	*robust, kräftig*
success	*Erfolg*
testimonial	*Zeugnis*
truthful	*wahrhaftig, ehrlich*
various	*verschieden(e)*
wilted	*verwelkt*
word-of-mouth advertising	*Mund-zu-Mund-Werbung*
words of farewell	*Abschiedsworte*
words of welcome	*Begrüßungsworte*

Words from the expert

Public relations specialists make flower arrangements of the facts, placing them so that the wilted and less attractive petals are hidden by sturdy blooms.
Alan Harrington

SPICE UP YOUR SPEECHES!*

Module 12

MAKE THAT SPEECH!

There are many forms of communication needed in a functioning company and one of these is the speech. This special type of presentation is usually performed by a senior member of the company. Very often speeches are made for fixed, special events. They also include typical forms of address and language. Hardman makes a mixture of several types of speech: He uses a toast, spices it with a pinch of motivation and adds a dash of criticism. Read on!

We focus on

- toasts and toasting
- effective speech-openers
- checklists for speakers
- and the voice as your medium

*Die Kunst der Rede in allen Geschäftssituationen erlernen Sie mit *Spice up your Speeches*, rororo sprachen 60804.

With a carrot and a stick

Busoom drifted on through the year. There were ups and downs. There were stresses and good times. At the beginning of December Hardman decided to fix the date for the Annual General Meeting. It was to be December 16th, just before Christmas. "But I'll make it a special meeting. I'll use it as a chance to tell them all the plain truth. And I'll motivate them to do better."
December 16th, in the production centre. (It was the only space big enough to accommodate 150 people). Hardman has a school bell on his rostrum which he rings vigorously. "Ladies and Gentleman, Ladies and Gentlemen, can I have your attention, please?" A hush descended over the assembled crowd.

Ladies and Gentlemen,

As you know it's my duty as well as an honour to hold a short speech every year about this time, to describe to you, the staff, how the company is faring in its different branches and businesses, and to say thank-you to you all for your efforts.
Of course, it's my privilege to propose the good health of the staff and I welcome the opportunity of saying a few words of thanks for your work during the year. Work can be a positive feature in our lives. It gives us a certain regularity. It gives us targets. And, it goes without saying that it creates the wherewithal to enable us to live the life we are accustomed to. I'm referring, of course, to salary, wages, income, whatever you prefer to call it.
And since I've arrived at the topic of work I feel I have to allow myself a few comments. They may not be popular. Work! Work can mean going to a workplace five days a week, eight hours per day. It may mean to some just putting in the hours to get their pay package at the end of the month. This type of worker is what we call here the "industrial civil servant". This person isn't productive. He or she doesn't actually row the boat forward. On the contrary, they hold it back, and they can sink it, too.

I know what I'm saying is not perhaps very encouraging, but it's the right time to bring it to the light of day. Especially now that I've had time to reflect on Busoom's business figures. Our figures have been up and down, but in the main the trend is not a positive one. Part of the explanation for this lies with technical matters such as currency rates and sales drives by our competitors etc. This is the normal business and perhaps we can't impact on that.
However, dear members of Busoom, I feel that overall there is a little bit of a lack of motivation, an attitude that things will "take care of themselves". This type of thinking has its own consequences in the various areas of our business. It can mean the parts for our doors don't fit perfectly, or a delivery to customer's site takes place one day late, or a telephone caller is frustrated by lack of service, etc. etc. etc. And the bottom line or the bill for this is that we lose customers. Or we don't even gain them. All this is a part of the reason why we are not doing well. It's all about operational excellence.
I'm aware you didn't expect to hear this. It's not typical for the AGM. My goal here is to identify a problem and to solve it with your help and suggestions. And now I'll come to the figures in some more detail ...

The Analyst's Corner

TASK 1: Sit back and think

Hardman was trying to communicate with his workforce.
Answer the following questions on this topic.

1. What does Hardman want to communicate with his opening?
2. What is the theme in the main body of Hardman's speech?
3. What is Hardman's real goal in talking about work?
4. What techniques does he use to emphasise that he is speaking and not reading his speech?
5. Can you find two points which add imagery to the speech to bring it alive?

WORKING with the language

TASK 2: Business phrases to remember

Währungskurse	________ rates
Kunden verlieren	________ customers
Zeit investieren	________ in time
Wir können das nicht beeinflussen.	We can't ________ on that.
den Termin für eine Besprechung festsetzen	________ a ________ for a meeting.
seine Lohntüte bekommen	______ one's ______ ______
Das Produktionszentrum fasst 150 Menschen.	The production centre ________ 150 people.
Werbefeldzug der Konkurrenten	sales ________ by ________

TASK 3: Beef up your word power

Find the opposite.

There were ups	and ________
we lose customers	we ________ customers
we are doing well	we are doing ________
a delivery is one day late	a delivery is one day ________
hush a scandal up	bring it to the ______ of ______

TASK 4: Streamlining the English

Do you remember the way Hardman put it?

I think everybody knows	______ ______ ______ know
the consequence is	the ________ line is
it is self-evident	it ______ without ______
just wait and see	things will ______ ______ ______ themselves
I'll give you the exact figures later	I'll come to the figures in ______ ______ ______ later

The Communicator's corner (1)

Proposing a toast

The toast to the staff, to a contract or to a guest is a standard speech in business life. First, we'll give you an idea as to the structure of a toast, then we'll provide you with a few useful phrases.

The opening

The first sentence is easy: "I have been asked to propose the health of ... Nothing gives me greater pleasure." Anyone can get that far!
Compliment entry: Say how honoured you are to be asked to speak. Pay compliments to whoever should be thanked among the audience.

The middle

What is to go in the middle? Think first of what you are trying to achieve. Choose one or two themes. Talk about the atmosphere and the working climate, the good relationship with the business partner.
You then throw in a suitable quotation or some humorous advice.

The close

One good thing about a toast is that you don't have to worry about how to end the speech. You simply invite the audience to drink with you, and your closing words are a variation of "Please raise your glasses to our guests of honour."

Time for a smile

"I wrote that speech myself," he told his boss.
"It's nice of you to take the blame," his boss replied.

Keywords in 'toasting'

Toasting persons

It is my privilege and pleasure to propose the health of ...	*Es ist mir eine Ehre und ein Vergnügen, auf das Wohl von ... anzustoßen.*
I have been asked to propose the health of ... Nothing gives me greater pleasure.	*Ich bin gebeten worden, mit Ihnen auf das Wohl von ... zu trinken. Ich tue das mit dem größten Vergnügen.*
I'd like to make a toast to our new colleague.	*Ich möchte einen Toast auf unseren neuen Kollegen ausbringen.*
I rise to toast our guests.	*Ich erhebe mich, um auf das Wohl unserer Gäste zu trinken.*

Drinking to business situations

I'd like to propose a toast to the conclusion of our contract.	*Ich schlage vor, wir stoßen auf den Abschluss unseres Vertrags an.*
Let's raise our glasses to the future of the company.	*Erheben wir unsere Gläser und trinken auf die Zukunft der Firma.*
Let's celebrate our success with a glass of champagne.	*Begießen wir unseren Erfolg mit einem Glas Champagner.*

Closing the toast

Here's to the company!	*Auf das Wohl der Firma!*
To your good health!	*Auf Ihr Wohl!*
Cheers!	*Prost!*

What not to say to the speaker

Anyone who told you to be yourself couldn't have given you worse advice.

❖

I'll never forget your speech – although I'll keep trying.

❖

Scientists claim that the average person speaks 10,000 words a day. You're far above average.

The Communicator's Corner (2)

Checklist 1: Preparing the speech

Before you start writing you should have a clear answer to these questions:

1. Why was I asked to deliver the speech? What is the occasion?
2. How will the place and the hour of the speech affect its content?
3. What is the subject of my speech?
4. How long am I supposed to speak?
5. Will there be a previous speaker talking about the same theme? Should I get in touch with him?

Checklist 2: Getting to know the audience

1. What are the education, functions, sex of my listeners?
2. What age group do they belong to?
3. What do they already know about my subject?
4. What do they expect of my speech?
5. How can I compliment my audience?

Checklist 3: Drafting the speech

1. What is my purpose? What is my message? What are my arguments? Do I want to inform, to entertain, to persuade or to motivate?
2. How do I appeal to the audience? Shall I appeal to logic, emotions, needs, fears?
3. How am I going to organise the parts of my speech? Chronologically, by cause and effect, with problem and solution, from weaker arguments to stronger arguments?
4. Do I have a good opening? A proverb, a joke, an anecdote, hot news?
5. What is going into the body of my speech? Comparisons, contrasts, examples, facts, statistics, testimony by authorities?
6. How can I conclude my speech?

Checklist 4: Rehearsing the speech

Use a mirror and a tape recorder.

1. Am I talking too low, too loud, too fast?
2. Where do I pause for effect?
3. How do I guide their attention?
4. Do I vary the tone of my voice?
5. Do I use body language?
6. When do I need audio-visual support?

Checklist 5: Watching the audience

Observe your audience, get feedback and adapt to their reactions.

1. Do they understand me?
2. Do I give them time to follow?
3. Do I keep eye contact?
4. Shall I skip dry facts and figures?
5. Am I keeping to my outline?
6. Am I within the time limit?

Nine effective speech openers

1. The shock tactic introduction

Some speakers shock or provoke their listeners in order to wake up a department that had fallen into a comfortable habit of taking things too easy. Careful! You have to know your audience well enough to calculate the risks of this method. Here's an example:
"Ladies and Gentlemen, the rumour is going around that HQ will introduce lean management and might lay off 1,500 employees."

2. The "That's-me-opening"

What to do if there is no host to introduce you or if he has forgotten to do so? Use the "That's me" opening: Project a photo of a baby. "That's me when I took my first degree. Let me tell you a bit about this baby ..."

3. The rhetorical question

It is one of the most common and most effective ways of opening a speech. It creates a link between you and the listeners. It involves them because they immediately begin to frame an answer, and then listen closely to see if their answer matches yours.
"What can we compare this department to? A chicken yard, an ant hill? A yard full of chickens running around in all directions? Or a colony of ants, each with his own tasks, but responsible for and dedicated to the good of the community?"

4. The story

Imagine you had to speak before a group of marketing or sales people. Wouldn't this story be a good start for illustrating how difficult it can be to recognise sales opportunities?
Two shoe salesmen travelled on the same boat to West Africa, each representing different shoe companies. After landing they looked around, and what struck them first was the fact that all the natives were barefoot. The first salesman cabled his head office: "Nobody here wearing shoes. Coming home by next ship."
The second salesman cabled his boss: "Nobody here wearing shoes. Market is wide open."

5. The Anecdote

The following story could be used as an opening in a training seminar. Receptionists, waiters and policemen tend to judge people by their appearance, which can be a mistake – as this story illustrates:

One day, a shabby gentleman turned up at the National Gallery with a painting under his arm. He asked to see the director, but was rudely turned away, and only after he had waited patiently and repeated his request was he allowed in.

The old man tried to persuade the director to take a quick look, but he firmly refused and was on the verge of having him removed from the office when the covering fell off – revealing a masterpiece that the director had tried but failed to buy at an auction.

"My name is Sir William Wallace," said the shabby gentleman, a well known millionaire, quietly, "I came to offer this picture to the National Gallery."

6. Thanking your host for his flattering introduction

"Thank you for that kind introduction. It seems that I shall now have to say two prayers for forgiveness: the first for my host for telling so many lies in praising me; the second for myself – for enjoying it so much."

7. Quotable quotes

A quotation is both a good entry and exit. There are lots of dictionaries to provide you with quotes that will fit your theme. Don't use quotes to show off what you know. If you have forgotten the name of the author, try this: "A famous person once said" or "It has been said that ...".

8. The joke

It's effective but dangerous. First, it must be exactly on target for your message; second, it must suit the audience and the occasion; third, it can be a catastrophe if it falls flat and nobody laughs.

9. Complimenting the audience

"Ladies and Gentlemen, your presence proves that there are still many people who are ready to take responsibility for our environment."

Your voice as your medium

Your voice, tone, intonation, resonance, pauses and speed account for 84 percent of the credibility you have when people can't see you. This is the case when you talk on the telephone or record a text for a slide show or a multimedia website. Here is some advice for the rest of us who are no actors.

How to deliver the speech

Your voice is the primary vehicle to carry your message. It is like transport – you can have an old car that rattles along or a smooth running car. Both will get you to your destination, but the quality of the ride can vary greatly. The worst thing you can do is read your speech. Use notes and outlines of your main ideas when you speak. This will allow you to let your mind select words spontaneously and force your voice to be active, animated and natural because you are continuously thinking, adapting, and altering your content.

How fast should you speak?

You should be speaking at about 120 to 150 words per minute. Find out by timing yourself. However, this rate is not uniform like the tick-tock of a clock. Good speakers present main ideas and difficult points at a slower pace than they do a joke. Follow these rules of thumb:

Theme	Rate of speech
complex or serious	more slowly
humorous or exciting	more quickly

Emphasise the right word

Take the sentence "We will make it our business to listen to our customer's feedback". Read it, emphasising a different word each time. Notice the difference in the meaning, depending on which word you emphasise. Experiment, emphasising the right word in your everyday conversations.

Pause for effect

You can pause naturally for three to four seconds, even in the middle of a sentence. The problem is we are not used to doing it. When we do it, a three or four-second pause seems like twenty seconds in our own minds. Practise pausing and getting feedback to learn how natural you sound when you pause.

How to practise

The best exercise for developing your vocal skills is to record yourself. Do it as often as possible. Record a telephone conversation, a business meeting, a conversation with a friend, etc. Even record casual conversations using a dictaphone. The most important way for you to improve your voice is to get audio feedback.

WORD AID

account for 84 percent	*84 Prozent ausmachen*
adequate	*angemessen*
advice	*Rat*
affect	*beeinflussen*
AGM (Annual General Meeting)	*jährliche Gesamtkonferenz / Vollversammlung*
animated	*lebhaft*
ant hill	*Ameisenhaufen*
appeal to logic	*die Logik ansprechen*
appearance	*Äußeres*
assemble	*sich versammeln*
attitude	*Einstellung, Haltung*
average	*Durchschnitt*
bottom line; the ~ is	*das Ende vom Lied ist ...*
carrot and stick	*Zuckerbrot und Peitsche*
casual	*lässig*

choice of words	*Wortwahl*
civil servant	*Beamte(r)*
claim	*behaupten, beanspruchen*
contract	*Vertrag*
credibility	*Glaubwürdigkeit*
currency rates	*Währungskurse*
customer's site	*Kundenstandort*
dedicated	*engagiert*
deliver a speech	*eine Rede halten*
delivery	*Lieferung*
depend on	*abhängen von*
destination	*Ziel; Bestimmungsort*
disarm arguments	*Argumente entschärfen*
drift	*treiben*
duty	*Pflicht*
effort	*Anstrengung*
emphasise	*betonen*
fare (old-fashioned)	*sich befinden*
gain customers	*Kunden gewinnen*
goal	*Ziel*
habit	*Gewohnheit*
hush; a ~ descends over the crowd	*Schweigen legt sich über die Menge*
male	*männlich*
opportunity	*Gelegenheit*
outline	*Gliederung*
persuade	*überreden*
plain truth	*nackte Wahrheit*
previous; the ~ speaker	*der Vorredner*
propose the good health	*auf jemandes Gesundheit trinken*
proposing a toast	*einen Toast/Trinkspruch ausbringen*
proverb	*Sprichwort*
quotation	*Zitat*
rate	*Geschwindigkeit*
record	*aufnehmen, aufzeichnen (Tonband)*
refer to	*sich beziehen auf*

reflect on	*nachdenken über*
rehearse	*proben, üben*
request	*Bitte*
rule of thumb	*Daumenregel*
sales drive	*Werbekampagne*
shabby	*ärmlich, heruntergekommen*
smooth	*ruhig, sanft*
speech	*Rede*
suited for	*passen, angebracht sein für*
take into account	*berücksichtigen*
take the blame	*die Schuld auf sich nehmen*
target	*Ziel*
used to doing	*gewohnt, etwas zu tun*
verge; be on the ~of doing	*nahe daran sein, etwas zu tun*
vigorous(ly)	*kräftig*
wage package	*Lohntüte*
wherewithal	*Mittel, Geld*

What not to say to the speaker

Of course I'm listening to you; didn't you hear me yawning?

❖

I've enjoyed listening to you. My mind needed a rest.

MASTER YOUR MEETINGS*

Module 13

MEETINGS SMOOTH AND LIGHT

It has been said that some companies spend as much as seventy percent of their time holding meetings. And, it seems that at least a large part of these corporate "rendezvous" are a waste of time. The first question to answer: "Is the meeting really necessary, and what is the real purpose of it?" If the answer is "yes", then how do we manage the meeting so that it succeeds?

We focus on

- how to conduct meetings
- the terms and phrases used in meetings

*If you want to know more about how to master meetings read *Get Through at Meetings, Business English für Konferenzen und Präsentationen*, rororo sprachen 60262.

Meetings smooth and light – Busoom's best

Mr Seaweed (**S**), who recently visited a special seminar on running meetings, is in the chair. He calls the attendees to order. Present are the head of sales, Mr Pushit (**P**), and Mr Buyit (**B**), after-sales.

S: Gentlemen, Gentlemen, in my capacity as personnel director I'd like to officially open this meeting. You will have received my invitation, plus the minutes of the last "department leader" meeting. You'll have had time to prepare your status reports and requirements. Today's agenda is concerned with your departmental training needs. I'll preside over the meeting. Mr Pushit could you take the minutes? We'll use the beamer and the OHP. Thanks. So, to come to the first item on the agenda today, which is telephone training. Mr Pushit, let's begin with you.

P: Actually, we have no requirement.

B: John, that simply can't be right. I've heard from both customers and staff that some of your staff behave like monkeys on the phone. You're famous for it.

P: Just a moment, just a moment. Before you slag off my staff I suggest you look in your own backyard.

B: What on earth ...

S: Gentlemen, will both of you take a step back. Mr Pushit, we have money in our budget for three trainings per salesman. You've got fifteen salesmen, and five sales support. Are they all perfect? I wish my people were.

P: Well, since you put it like that, of course not.

S: I can imagine your problem is that your people shouldn't be seen to be going on an introductory telephone training?

P: Yes, that's about it.

S: Well, they've a potential of three each. Let's offer them a middle-level training, and in some individual cases advanced training.

P: Okay. I would need ten middle-levels and three advanced.

S: Great! Mr Buyit, your forecast.

B: Three beginners, six middles and three advanced.

S: Okay. If that point is done I'd like to ... (*fade out*) (*fade in*) ... Right. I'm just looking at the clock and I must bring our meeting to order. We're over time. I'd like to make a brief summary of the items we agreed on today. Firstly, the topic was training and the various extra things we have on offer. Item one was telephone training. We had twenty-five seminars. Next was specialised training in presentations, negotiations and sales. The decision was two courses weekly to cover the needs of all three departments together. We also ... (*fade out*)

(*fade in*) ... and so finally I'd like to nominate you, Mr Pushit, to deal with the two "to dos". Let's now draw the meeting to a close. The next meeting will be on June 5th. Thank you.

The following day in Hardman's office.

H: How did your requirements meeting go yesterday?

S: Not much to shout about. They weren't really prepared for it. It was like getting blood out of a stone. I practically had to do it for them.

The Analyst's Corner

TASK 1: Did you get the message?

Meetings should be a question of clear communication.

1. How do you know Seaweed organises meetings with good communication in mind?
2. What indicates that he is a good chairman?
3. Where can we recognise positive manipulation on the part of Seaweed?
4. How does Seaweed indicate he is about to close the meeting?

Time for a smile

If Moses had held meetings,
the Israelites would still be in Egypt.

WORKING with the language

TASK 2: Some steps in meetings

eine Einladung erhalten	________ an invitation
um Ruhe bitten	________ to order
die Besprechung eröffnen	________ the meeting
das Protokoll führen	________ the ________
eine Besprechung wieder in geordnete Bahnen lenken	________ a meeting to ________
der erste Tagesordnungspunkt	the first ________ on the ________
eine Besprechung schließen	________ the meeting to a ________

TASK 3: In other words

Do you remember the alternatives in our dialogue?

head of selling	head of ________
customer service	________
participant at a meeting	________
be in the chair	________ a meeting / ________ over the meeting

The true nature of meetings

A meeting is a group of men who individually can do nothing, but together can decide that nothing can be done.

Fred Allen

The Communicator's Corner

Some useful phrases you might need at meetings*

1. *Die Eröffnung* – The opening

Meine Damen und Herren, ich erkläre die Sitzung für eröffnet.	Ladies and Gentlemen, I declare the meeting open.
Meine Damen und Herren, darf ich die Konferenz nun eröffnen?	Ladies and Gentlemen, may I open this conference now?
Ich freue mich, Sie heute alle begrüßen zu dürfen.	I'm happy to welcome all of you today.
Ich darf die Verspätung von Direktor X entschuldigen.	May I apologise for the fact that Director X is held up by urgent business?

How to maintain discipline

"There are two sides to every question," said the new boss at the first meeting, "my side and the wrong side. And don't say 'yes' until I've finished."

2. *Die Tagesordnung* – The agenda

Haben alle eine Kopie der Tagesordnung erhalten?	Has everyone received a copy of the agenda?
Möchte jemand noch einen Punkt auf die Tagesordnung setzen?	Does anybody wish to add an item / point to the agenda?
Ich schlage vor, der Tagesordnung folgende Punkte hinzuzufügen.	I'd like to suggest / propose that we add the following items to the agenda.
Könnten wir Punkt 3 der Tagesordnung streichen?	Could we delete item 3 from the agenda?

*More phrases in *Master your Business Phrases*, rororo sprachen 60725, and *Get Through at Meetings*, rororo sprachen 60262.

3. *Das Protokoll* – The minutes

Haben alle das Protokoll eingesehen?	Has everybody seen the minutes?
Können wir das Protokoll als angenommen betrachten?	Can we take the minutes as read?
Wer führt heute das Protokoll?	Who is going to keep the minutes today?
Wer ist heute der Protokollant?	Who's today's minute-taker?

Food for thought

A committee is a group that keeps the minutes and loses the hours.
Milton Berle

4. *Den Zweck erläutern* – Explaining the purpose

Wie Sie der Tagesordnung entnehmen ...	As you can see from the agenda ...
Thema unserer Besprechung ist ...	The subject of our meeting is ...
Unsere Aufgabe ist es, Empfehlungen über ... zu erarbeiten.	The task before us is to come up with recommendations on ...
Heute müssen drei Entscheidungen gefällt werden.	There are three decisions to be taken today.

Why meetings fail

The last time I sat in at a meeting we were presented with a plan which had two alternatives. We therefore narrowed it down to eighteen possibilities for further discussion.

TASK 4: How good is your memory?

Translate the terms in brackets.

1. May I (*sich entschuldigen*) for the fact that Director X is (*aufhalten*) by urgent business?
2. I'd like to (*vorschlagen*) that we add the following (*Punkte*) to the (*Tagesordnung*).
3. Could we (*streichen*) item 3?
4. We (*betrachten / voraussetzen*) the (*Protokoll*) (*als angenommen*).
5. As you can see from the agenda there are three (*Entscheidungen*) to be (*treffen*) today.

Why meetings fail

A committee is twelve men
doing the work of one.

5. *Meinungen sammeln* – Collecting opinions

Ich würde gerne eure Meinungen zu ... hören.	I'd like to hear your views on ...
Möchtest du vielleicht etwas dazu sagen, Tina?	I wonder if you'd like to comment, Tina?
Und wie stehen Sie zu dieser Frage, Dr. Brain?	And where exactly do you stand on this issue, Dr Brain?
Ich möchte gern Herrn Brown das Wort erteilen.	I'd like to give the floor to Mr Brown.
Ich glaube, unser Buchhalter möchte dazu Stellung nehmen.	I think our accountant would like to make a point.

The true nature of meetings

The average meeting comprises eight executives,
each of whom wishes that at least three of the other
seven weren't on it. *Harvard Business Review*

6. *Probleme vertagen* – Putting off problems

Wir können das vielleicht zu einem späteren Zeitpunkt besprechen.	Perhaps we can discuss that at a later date.
Ich schlage vor, wir heben uns diese Angelegenheit für die nächste Besprechung auf.	I suggest we leave this matter until our next meeting.
Wenn niemand Einwände erhebt, schlage ich vor, wir verschieben diesen Punkt, bis wir die neuesten Zahlen haben.	If nobody has any objections, I propose we postpone this item till we get the latest figures.
Wenn Sie einverstanden sind, verschieben wir diese Sache, bis uns mehr Informationen zur Verfügung stehen.	If you agree, I propose we defer this matter until we have more information at our disposal.
Könnten wir die Besprechung auf Montag vertagen?	Could we adjourn the meeting to Monday?

TASK 5: Do you remember these?

Put these words into the sentences.

date	point	issue
make	stand	adjourn
later	to	on

1. And where exactly do you _________ __ this ______ , Bob?
2. Could we _________ the meeting ______ Monday?
3. Perhaps we can discuss that at a _________ _________ .
4. I think our accountant would like to _________ a _________ .

7. *Abstimmen lassen* – Putting it to the vote

Stimmen wir darüber ab.	Let's have a vote on this. / Let's put it to the vote.
Könnten wir darüber abstimmen?	Could we move to a vote on it?
Vielleicht sollten wir in aller Form darüber abstimmen.	Perhaps we should take a formal vote on this.
Darf ich um Handzeichen bitten?	Can I ask for a show of hands?
Wer dafür ist, möge die Hand heben.	Those in favour raise their hands.
Wer ist dagegen?	Those against?
Wer enthält sich der Stimme?	Any abstentions?
Der Antrag ist mit sieben zu vier Stimmen angenommen.	The motion is carried by seven votes to four.
Der Antrag ist mit acht zu drei Stimmen abgelehnt.	The motion is rejected by eight votes to three.

Time for a smile

Once the chairman of the Board of Directors visited one of his directors in hospital. "Bob," he said, "the Board of Directors wishes you a speedy recovery – and it was a majority decision of seven to five."

8. *Die Sitzung ist beendet* – The meeting is closed

Gut, ich glaube, wir haben alles besprochen.	Well, I think we've covered everything.
Nun, damit haben wir die Tagesordnung abgeschlossen.	Well, I think that completes our agenda.
Damit wäre unser Geschäft für heute erledigt. Vielen Dank.	That concludes our business for today. Thank you.
Wenn niemand mehr etwas zu sagen hat, würde ich die Besprechung gern schließen.	If nobody has anything to add, I'd like to draw the meeting to an end.
Ich möchte allen für ihre konstruktiven Beiträge danken.	I'd like to thank everyone for their constructive contributions.
Ich erkläre die Sitzung für geschlossen.	I declare the meeting closed.

TASK 6: What about these?

Translate and fit them in, but mind the form of the words.

heben	*beenden*	*ablehnen*
Enthaltung	*Stimmen*	*erklären*

1. Those in favour __________ their hands.
2. Any __________ ?
3. The motion is __________ by eight __________ to three.
4. I __________ the meeting __________ .

TASK 7: Beef up your word power

invite to a meeting	*c* _____ a meeting
discuss all the topics	*c* ______ all the topics
suggest a strategy	*p* _________ a strategy
adjourn a meeting	*p* _________ a meeting
cancel an item on the agenda	*d* _______ an item

Synergy

In a heartless but clever move, the owners of a large mail order diet pill business with thousands of clients sold their mailing list to a quality chocolate company. The company's sales rose by 300 percent. So did the diet pill company's sales a few weeks later.

The Psychologist's Corner

Why meetings fail – Communication problems and how to solve them

Meetings fail when the participants cannot or do not want to communicate. There are three big problems that most participants have with communication. Know them and avoid them.

Wrong attitudes

- Participants come unprepared and cannot contribute.
- They talk to impress the audience instead of communicating with each other.
- Or they are not interested in an exchange of views, but try to trip their partners up instead of trying to strike a compromise.
- They talk in order to convince and to persuade those who listen.

They do not or cannot listen

- They are flooded with information by a speaker.
- They cannot pay attention because they are busy thinking about what they are going to say next.
- They only pay attention to those speakers they agree with.

Misunderstandings

- They do not speak the same language.
- They misinterpret body language.
- Even if they speak the same language, they misinterpret the meaning of words.

How to avoid problems

- Arrange some counselling for the different employees.
- Don't call a meeting at four o'clock on Friday, when people are tired and looking forward to their weekend.
- Select participants according to problem and limit their number.
- Send the agenda to the attendees well in advance so that they can suggest changes or additions to it and prepare contributions.

- A good chairperson keeps discipline and calls undisciplined participants to order.
- Avoid all possible interruptions. Go to a conference room or switch on the answering machine.
- Distribute the minutes within a day or two.
- At each meeting, approve the minutes of the previous meeting and verify their accuracy with the attendees.
- Offer training seminars on how to conduct meetings efficiently.

Time for a smile

A science graduate asks, "Why does it work?" An engineering graduate asks, "How does it work?" A business graduate asks, "How much will it cost?" A media studies graduate asks, "Do you want fries with it?"

WORD AID

accuracy	*Genauigkeit, Korrektheit*
advance; in ~	*im Voraus*
advanced training	*Fortgeschrittenentraining*
after-sales / customer service	*Kundendienst*
agenda	*Tagesordnung*
answering machine	*Anrufbeantworter*
approve the minutes	*das Protokoll billigen, absegnen*
attendee	*Teilnehmer*
attention; pay ~	*aufmerksam sein*
average	*Durchschnitts-; Durchschnitt*
bring a meeting to order	*eine Besprechung wieder in geordnete Bahnen lenken*
backyard; look in one's own ~	*vor seiner eigenen Tür kehren*
call to order	*um Ruhe bitten*

chair a meeting / be in the chair	*den Vorsitz führen, eine Besprechung leiten*
conduct meetings	*Konferenzen leiten, durchführen*
contribute	*einen Beitrag leisten*
convince	*überzeugen*
cram	*stopfen*
defuse the situation	*die Situation entschärfen*
dos (do's); the to-dos	*die nötigen Schritte*
draw the meeting to a close	*eine Besprechung schließen*
fail	*fehlschlagen, Misserfolg werden*
famous for	*berühmt für*
sales support	*Verkaufspersonal im Innendienst*
flight attendant	*Flugbegleiter(in)*
flooded	*überflutet*
forecast	*Prognose, Vorhersage, Schätzung*
fries	*Pommes*
further discussion	*weitere Diskussion*
get blood out of a stone	*einen Stein erweichen*
head of sales / purchasing	*Einkaufsleiter*
in my capacity as	*in meiner Eigenschaft als*
indicate	*andeuten*
introductory training	*Einführungskurs*
item; the first ~ on the agenda	*der erste Tagesordnungspunkt*
look forward to	*sich freuen auf*
lug	*zerren, schleppen*
middle-level training	*Kurs auf mittlerem Niveau*
minutes	*Protokoll*
monkey	*Affe*
move; a clever ~	*ein kluger Schachzug*
narrow alternatives down	*Alternativen eingrenzen*
not much to shout about	*nicht das Gelbe vom Ei*
open the conference	*die Konferenz eröffnen*
persuade	*überreden*
receive an invitation	*eine Einladung erhalten*
recently	*kürzlich, vor kurzem*
recovery	*Wiedergenesung*
requirement	*Anforderung, Bedarf*

run a meeting	*eine Besprechung leiten*
sales	*Umsatz*
slag someone off	*jemanden beleidigen / heruntermachen*
speedy recovery	*schnelle Genesung*
status report	*Bericht über den letzten Stand*
strike a compromise	*einen Kompromiss schließen*
take a step back	*zurückstecken*
take the minutes	*das Protokoll führen*

Time for a smile

A Scottish businessman was having a hard time lugging his oversized travel bag onto the plane. With the aid of a flight attendant, he finally managed to cram it into the overhead cupboard. "Do you always carry such heavy luggage?" she sighed. "Never again," the man replied. "Next time, I'm going in the bag."

Module 14

SMALL TALK FOR BETTER BUSINESS*

BUSOOM GRAPEVINE

Communication, which in this case means clear, warm positive communication, is the key to success. It's also decisive in the working environment. As we've mentioned before there are many interfaces where communication can occur – the e-mail, letter, presentation, in a speech, at a briefing, face-to-face with colleagues etc. And one underrated but vital area of communication is small talk. Some people even say this vehicle is the most important one for circulating business information around the company.

We focus on

- how to be a good small-talker
- how to be a good networker
- useful phrases for small-talkers

*Kennen Sie das ultimative Rowohlt-Taschenbuch zu diesem Kapitel? *Small Talk for Big Business. Business Conversation für bessere Kontakte*; rororo sprachen 60577.

Busoom Grapevine

Mrs Velvet (**V**) has been with Busoom almost six weeks. She is looking for connections with worthwhile Busoomers. She also needs to become part of the Busoom grapevine. This is where most of the company information is passed around. Using this mechanism she can find out what the real attitude to management decisions is. But first things first! Velvet is talking to Mrs Friendly (**F**), a girl in her early thirties. They are at the same table in the canteen.

V: So you've been working here for three years, Mrs Friendly. You're not from this area, are you?
F: No, I'm not, actually. I'm from Wapperdale in the north.
V: Really, That's interesting. I went to polytechnic in Wapperdale[1].
F: Did you? It's a small world, isn't it? But you were saying earlier you've had problems to get to know people here at the company.
V: Yes, it's been a bit of a problem. I've probably got strange hobbies. For example, I play squash as often as I can.
F: Oh, that's interesting. So do I. I play in a league here[2]. Perhaps we could have a game together. What sort of level are you?
V: Well, I've been playing for six years.
F: Just like me. Well, ... (*fade out*)

A few days later at the squash club.

V: Phew, that was a hard game. I really enjoyed it.
F: Yes, you were far better than I thought.
V: But it makes this Lager taste all the better.
F: I suppose you need to let off steam with the type of job you've got.
V: How do you mean? Your work is just as stressful, I guess.
F: Yes, but I mean working close to Hardman. It can't be easy.
V: Oh, he's okay. His bark is worse than his bite. But it's difficult for him to make decisions that the workforce understands. Look at the rule about smoking and alcohol in the company. I bet that went down really badly[3].

1 The numbers in the text refer to the questions in Task 1 (The Analyst's Corner).

F: Well, you'd be surprised, actually Ellen. I think most of us understood the reasons for all that. Most of us also want to do our work and not to lose days because of feeling ill on the next day.

V: I'm pretty sure that Mr Hardman doesn't know that. I'm sure he'd be surprised.

F: Maybe. Hey, you said you lived in Wapperdale a few years ago[4].

V: Did I? Oh yes, I had a great time especially in Wapperdale Alberfield. I remember there were some great pubs in Alberfield. We used to ... (*fade out*)

So you see, there are many ways to make contact with people in an easy and relaxed way. It's not just a matter of talking about the weather. Indeed every person who talks to another somehow has his own "agenda" or reason for communicating with another person. In small-talking you have to find common ground for communication. It might be talking about common memories, finding things you both do, or simply avoiding hurting your conversation partner. It's all to do with small-talking.

The Analyst's Corner

TASK 1: Reading between the lines

1. Why does Velvet mention that she went to the polytechnic?
2. What technique is being used at point 2 in the dialogue?
3. What is Velvet's intention in her comment at point 3?
4. Friendly mentions Wapperdale again. Why?

WORKING with the language

TASK 2: Get your verb forms right

1. I (*work*) at Busoom's for almost six weeks.
2. At the moment I (*work*) close to Hardman.
3. I (*look*) for connections with worthwhile Busoomers.
4. I (go) to polytech in Wapperdale.
5. I (*play)* squash for six years.
6. I (*play)*) as often as I can.

TASK 3: Streamline your English

Do you remember the phrases in the text?

Do it if you want to be successful.	This is the ________ to success
The world is a village.	It's a ________ world, ________?
He got rid of his aggressions.	He ________ off ________.
He's a rough diamond, but he's good at heart.	His ________ is worse than his ________.
The new rule wasn't taken well.	It ________ ________ badly.

The Communicator's Corner (1)

1. Starting a conversation with strangers

Entschuldigung, ist dieser Platz besetzt?	Excuse me, is this seat taken?
Ein scheußliches Wetter, nicht wahr?	Nasty weather, isn't it?
Sind Sie zum ersten Mal in Deutschland?	Is this your first visit to Germany?
Sind Sie geschäftlich hier oder zum Vergnügen?	Are you here on business or pleasure?

2. At a congress or a conference

Entschuldigen Sie, wo ist das Konferenzzimmer?	Excuse me, where is the conference room?
Kennen Sie den Gastredner?	Do you happen to know the guest speaker?
Wie lange bleiben Sie? – Nur für zwei Tage.	How long are you staying? – Just two days.
Wir könnten zusammen zu Abend essen, wenn Sie wollen.	We could have dinner together, if you like.

3. Introducing yourself

Übrigens, ich heiße Meier.	By the way, my name's Meier.
Ich sollte mich vielleicht vorstellen. Mein Name ist Tom Dobson.	Perhaps I should introduce myself. Tom Dobson's the name.
Ich bin aus Bonn. Wo kommen Sie her?	I'm from Bonn. Where are you from?
Ich bin auf Urlaub / Geschäftsreise hier.	I am here on a holiday / business trip?
Freut mich, Sie kennen zu lernen.	Pleased to meet you.

TASK 4: Let's take the first steps

Imagine this dialogue at the congress centre.

Sie fragen, …	**Er /sie antwortet, dass …**
wo der Konferenzraum ist.	er im zweiten Stock ist.
ob der Stuhl frei ist.	er frei ist.
wer der Gastredner ist.	er ihn auch nicht kennt.
wie lange Ihr Nachbar bleibt.	er zwei Tage bleibt.

4. Ice breakers

Ich hoffe, Sie hatten eine(n) gute(n) Reise (Flug).	I hope you had a good /pleasant journey (flight).
Der Zug war ziemlich überfüllt.	The train was rather overcrowded.
Der Flug war ziemlich unruhig.	The flight was rather bumpy.
Haben Sie unsere Firma gleich gefunden?	Did you find our company straight away?
Darf ich Ihnen etwas zum Trinken anbieten?	May I offer you something to drink?
Ich nehme das Gleiche wie Sie.	I'll have the same as you.

5. Be my guest

Haben Sie schon etwas für heute Abend vor?	Have you got anything planned for tonight?
Möchten Sie heute Abend zu uns zum Essen kommen?	Would you like to join us for dinner this evening?
Vielen Dank, das ist sehr nett von Ihnen.	Thank you, that sounds very nice.
Hätten Sie und Ihre Frau Lust, heute Abend auf ein Glas Wein zu uns zu kommen?	Would you and your wife like to come over for a glass of wine?
Ich würde sehr gern, aber ich habe schon eine Verpflichtung.	I'd love to, but I've got another engagement.

6. Conversation openers

Waren Sie schon mal in England?	Have you been to England before?
Wie lange sind Sie schon in England?	How long have you been in England?
Ich bin seit drei Tagen in England.	I've been in England for three days.
Haben Sie sich schon eingelebt?	Have you adjusted to life here yet?
Die Menschen sind alle ausgesprochen freundlich.	The people are all really friendly.
Die Altstadt ist wirklich wundervoll.	The ancient city is really marvellous.
Wir können uns beim Essen weiter unterhalten.	We can continue our conversation at dinner.

TASK 5: Let's break the ice

Ask your question	He / she answers
Did you ....?	No, the flight was rather bumpy.
May I ....?	I'll have the same as you.
Would you .... dinner this evening?	I'd love to, but I've got an another engagement.
How long ....?	I've been in England for three days.

7. Suggesting a toast

Prost	Cheers!
Auf Ihr Wohl!	To your good health!
Ich schlage vor, wir trinken auf den Abschluss unseres Vertrags.	I'd like to propose a toast to the conclusion of our contract.
Erheben wir unsere Gläser und trinken auf die Zukunft Europas.	Let's raise our glasses to the future of Europe.
Ich möchte einen Toast auf unseren neuen Kollegen ausbringen.	I'd like to make a toast to our new colleague.
Meine Damen und Herren, begießen wir es mit einem Glas Champagner.	Ladies and Gentlemen, let's celebrate this with a glass of champagne.

8. Making polite noises

Das war wirklich ausgezeichnet.	That was really excellent.
Sie müssen mir das Rezept geben.	You must let me have the recipe.
Was für einen hübschen Garten Sie haben!	What a beautiful garden you have!
Herzlichen Glückwunsch zu Ihrem Geburtstag.	Many happy returns!

9. Exploring business opportunities

Sie scheinen eine Menge darüber zu wissen.	You seem to know a lot about these things.
Sie scheinen ein Experte in ... zu sein.	You seem to be an expert on ...
Sie müssen viel Erfahrung haben mit ...	You must have a lot of experience with ...
Ich glaube, wir können voneinander lernen.	I think we can learn from each other.
Unsere Geschäftsinteressen scheinen sich zu überlappen.	Obviously our business interests overlap in some areas.
Ich glaube, das ist in meinem und in Ihrem Interesse.	I think this is in my interest as well as yours.
Eine Hand wäscht die andere.	You scratch my back and I'll scratch yours.

10. Leave-taking

Mein Gott, ist es schon so spät?	Goodness, is it that time already?
Ich fürchte ich muss nun gehen.	I'm afraid I've got to leave now.
Ich fürchte, ich muss mich langsam auf den Weg machen.	I'm afraid I must be setting off now.
Aber Sie sind doch gerade erst gekommen.	But you've only just arrived.
Ich muss meinen Zug erreichen.	I've got a train to catch.
Wie schade, dass Sie schon gehen müssen.	Such a pity you have to go already.
Nun, ich will Sie nicht aufhalten.	Well, mustn't keep you.
Ich habe morgen einen anstrengenden Tag vor mir.	Tomorrow is going to be a hard day for me.
Es war ein bezaubernder Abend.	It's been a delightful evening.
Vielen Dank. Es war ein sehr schöner Abend.	Thank you ever so much. This has been a most pleasant evening.
Vielen Dank für das ausgezeichnete Abendessen.	Thank you so much for the superb dinner.
Keine Ursache. Wir hoffen, es hat Ihnen gefallen.	Don't mention it. We hope you enjoyed yourself.

TASK 6: You are the host

Prosten Sie Ihrem Gast zu.	To ____________________!
Sie glauben, dass er Computerexperte ist.	You ______________ computers.
Deuten Sie an, dass sich Ihre Geschäftsinteressen teilweise überlappen.	Obviously our ____________ ______ ______ ______ areas.
Sagen Sie, dass eine Zusammenarbeit im beiderseitigen Interesse wäre.	I think ____________________ ____________________.

Time for a smile

Small talk makes your business partners feel at home, even though you wish they were.

The Communicator's Corner (2)

From small talk to network

What is small talk?

- It has a lot to do with EQ, the Emotional Quotient.
- It is has a lot to do with people skills.
- It is a social skill that can be learned.
- Small talk can be a valuable business skill that leads to great contacts and good contracts.

How to be a good small-talker

- Small-talkers take interest in other people.
- They engage in satisfying contact with people.
- They encourage others to participate.
- They exchange information and ideas with others.
- They are good listeners.
- They enjoy the moment and the company.
- They want to make other people feel comfortable.

Small talk skills

Good small-talkers don't follow rules. They find the right words naturally without being aware of it. The ability to create the right atmosphere, to find the right words at the right moment is what we call skills.

1. Create a friendly atmosphere

Good small-talkers enjoy the conversation and want their partners to enjoy it, too. Avoid direct personal compliments. First, because they are often insincere, second, they can be misunderstood as flattery. It's safer to praise your partner's country, secretary or car: "I take every opportunity to visit Britain with its variety of charms whenever I can."

2. Make your name memorable

You do it by dropping a 'brain anchor' into people's memory "Please call me Fritz. I think you have a famous cartoon character called Fritz?" or "My name is Kohl, in English it means cabbage." Thus you create a pleasant association between your name and a very popular English cartoon or well-known vegetable. It will help people to remember you.

3. Building a bridge, meeting them on common ground

After having been introduced, the next step is to find something to small talk about. No problem, you'll always find something you have in common with others: the service at the restaurant, the food, a hobby, the same car or the weather.

4. Take a stand to show your personality

Small talk means engaging in a satisfying exchange of ideas. Good small-talkers do not only talk about a topic, but about their relationship to that topic: they take a stand, they show that they have formed an opinion about it. Your opinions are part of your personality. Be honest! Nobody likes 'yes-men'. The most successful people in business are also the most interesting.

5. Shine but don't boast

In today's information and service economy, people are the product and information is the currency. Successful people are good at self-marketing. They act as it is in written in the Bible: Don't hide your light under a bushel. Eighty percent of success is letting the right people know what your strengths are. A good small-talker knows when the moment has come to do it in a modest and tactful way.

Types of small talk

1. Small talk without a purpose

We distinguish between three levels of small talk. The first is small talk pure, innocent small talk without any thought of how to profit by it professionally. It is small talk without a purpose.

2. Small talk with a purpose

Small talk is not only a social skill, but also a business skill. Business people engage in small talk with a purpose. They are always on the look-out for a new business opportunities. They create contacts through small talk with people they are professionally interested in.

3. Small talk for networking

It's not important what you know, but who you know. Small-talkers with a vision try to find a place in a network of partners who collect and exchange useful information over a longer period of time. The effective networker makes the most of his personal contacts. He wants to establish a network as a bridge to professional success and expand his network

How to be an efficient networker

1. Be visible – show up

Small talk skills are helpful in creating business opportunities. However, you might be playing on the wrong stage to the wrong audience. Choose the right stage and step forward into the limelight. If you have a good product, you market it; if you want your skills to be appreciated, you have to self-market your personality. "Eighty percent of success is showing up," says Woody Allen. We recommend two stages for building your visibility:

Be read in business magazines

- Send letters to the letters pages
- Offer book reviews
- Write articles
- Send a free copy of a magazine to which you have contributed to all network partners and decision-makers

Be noticed at meetings, conferences and congresses

- Say your name
- Ask a question
- Make a contribution
- Score a point
- Make contacts during coffee breaks

Remember, it's not so important what you know as who you know. And you must have something to give to them in order to get something from them. Networking is not manipulating people, but an honest exchange by which all network partners profit.

2. Prick up your ears

A group of students in the Mannheim area collected all the information that their fellow students spend hours searching for on the Internet. They then put it on a CD-ROM. It was a hit and resulted in a company. When listening to people you can often learn about the problems with products or services. Solving problems can be a source of new business ideas.

A. Collect information	B. Exploit this information
What do people complain about?	There is a better service / product you could offer.
What are the people's needs that haven't yet been met?	There are new products or services to discover.
Who is the lawyer in town who specialises in cases your company has to deal with?	You might need his services one day. Try to get his phone number.
Who might be useful for my business?	Offer free advice, services or resources. Seek a long-term relationship.

TASK 7: Small talk international

Some nations thrive in the cocktail party atmosphere, others do not. Some may be talking endlessly when they are among themselves, however, when they meet foreigners they are never sure what to talk about. You are German, you travel a lot, you have met people from other countries and we suppose that you have already made some contacts.
Which group of nations do you think is very good (**1**), good (**2**), average (**3**) or weak (**4**) when it comes to small talk with foreigners? Mark them from 1 to 4 and compare with our rating in the Key.

Nations	Mark
British, Americans	
Chinese, Russians	
French, Australians, Canadians	
Finns, Swedes, Japanese	
Mexicans, Peruvians, Argentinians	
Germans	

Time for a smile

The following story might help you a little with the rating:
James Peabody, director of a company in the Midlands, welcomed an important customer from Germany. "We're so pleased to have you with us. I do hope you'll enjoy your stay. On Monday night you'll be my guest at the club. You'll meet a lot of interesting people and there's a lot of drinking and ..."
"I'm sorry, sir," interrupted the German. "I don't drink."
"Oh really? Let me see. Tuesday night! You'll like that. We always have a dance. There are lots of pretty girls. You'll really enjoy that."
"No, sir," said the German. "I don't go in for that sort of thing."
"Really? Hmm ... excuse me if I'm being indiscreet. Are you homosexual?" asked Peabody.
"Certainly not, sir."
"What a pity! In that case you won't enjoy Friday night either."

WORD AID

acquainted with	*vertraut, bekannt mit*
anchor	*Anker*
aware; be ~ of something	*sich einer Sache bewusst sein*
bark	*Bellen*
bite	*Biss*
boast	*prahlen*
common ground	*Gemeinsamkeit(en)*
connection	*Anschluss*
conscious(ly)	*bewusst*
create a link	*eine Beziehung herstellen*
decisive	*entscheidend, ausschlaggebend*
environment	*Umgebung, Milieu*
exploit	*ausnutzen, ausbeuten*
first things first	*eins nach dem anderen*
flattery	*Schmeichelei*
grapevine	*Buschtrommel, Gerüchteküche*
go down badly	*schlecht ankommen / aufgenommen werden*
interface	*Schnittstelle,*
let off steam	*Dampf ablassen*
memories	*Erinnerungen*
mole	*Maulwurf*
occur	*geschehen, vorkommen*
participate	*teilnehmen*
recommend	*empfehlen*
shine	*glänzen*
source	*Quelle*
stage	*Bühne*
stand; take a ~	*Position beziehen*
unconsciously	*unbewusst*
underrate	*unterschätzen, unterbewerten*
vital	*wesentlich, wichtig*

HOW TO NEGOTIATE SUCCESSFULLY

Module 15

WIN-WIN WITH BUSOOM SUPPLIERS

Any sort of negotiation requires excellent communication skills. This is because it is necessary to show your proposals clearly and simply. On the other hand you have to be able to understand exactly what your partner is offering. The tools you need for this include being familiar with terminology, listening carefully, and expressing yourself precisely and positively.

We focus on

- phrases for negotiations
- how to overcome objections
- the tricks of professional negotiators

Win-win with Busoom suppliers

Mr Ramsch from Production is meeting Mr Slippery from Solid Metals Ltd. to discuss quantities and prices for parts for the new sliding door. The night before Ramsch is at home in front of a mirror practising his arguments for the discussion with Slippery[1]. He makes a plan of his strategy and he rehearses his proposals.

Nine o'clock at Busoom, in the Production conference room. Ramsch has prepared mineral water and a bowel of fruit. A pot of coffee is waiting on the table with two cups[2].

R: (*fade in*) ... so Mr Slippery, perhaps we could talk about quantities. Our prognosis for our Superslider is that Busoom will need three hundred frames per month starting in June. I've given you the specifications, you've had time to calculate the costs.

S: That's right, but there are problems in this special design and, of course, the low number of parts.

R: Dear old Slippery! We've known each other for a long time, haven't we? As I remember there've always been problems with parts and quantities. And we've always found a way. I think we can work together to find common success[3].

S: You're right of course, but quantities are quantities.

R: Absolutely. I've been thinking about your needs in quantities, too[4]. Listen, you supply us with parts for our other ranges, don't you? Well, we'll increase those quantities. But from your side we expect very reasonable prices for the new parts, even with our low quantities.

S: It sounds okay, but what price level do you have in mind? (*fade out ... twenty minutes later*)

R: Well, I'm glad we've agreed on that. There is another point I'd like to discuss today, though. It's the issue of internal quality control of parts at your end.

S: I think our checks meet all expectations. I don't see any problem.

---

1 The numbers in the text refer to the questions in Task 1.

R: I'm afraid there is a problem[5]. Too many parts are defective, about one in ten. And remember, we assemble at the customer's site so the customer gets wind of the problem.

S: I see. Well, I can suggest a more strict system of control back at the company.

R: Yes, I really propose you do that. But we have another strategy, too. The defects cost us too much. We'd prefer a system where you do the QC as you see fit, but we fix a new contract where the bottom line is that when there are flaws, you replace them free of charge.

S: Well, that can certainly be arranged ...

R: And in the case of a defect you compensate our lost time and ... (*fade out*)

The Analyst's Corner

TASK 1: Reading between the lines

1. What is the importance of Ramsch's activities at home?
2. What is behind Ramsch's hospitality here?
3. "... together to find common success." What is Ramsch's tactic with this sentence?
4. Why does Ramsch mention his supplier's needs?
5. In the present negotiation what is Ramsch's intention here beginning "I'm afraid ..."?

Time for a smile

A group of friends who went deer hunting separated into pairs for the day. That night, one hunter returned alone, staggering under a heavy deer. "Where's Harry?" asked another hunter. "He fainted a couple miles up the trail," Harry's partner answered. "You left him lying there alone and carried the deer back?" – "Well," said the hunter. "I figured no one is going to steal Harry."

WORKING with the language

TASK 2: Business phrases to remember

über die Preise diskutieren	______________ prices
vernünftige Preise erwarten	expect ______________ prices
die Mengen erhöhen	______________ the quantities
von einem Problem Wind bekommen	______________ wind of the problem
beim Kunden zusammenbauen	____________ at the customer's site
Schadensersatz für verlorene Zeit leisten	_____________ someone's lost time
fehlerhafte Teile umsonst ersetzen	______________ defective parts ____________ of __________

TASK 3: Beef up your word power

Find the corresponding nouns.

propose	make a ______________
supply spare parts	be a ______________ of spare parts
specify the measurements and tolerances	the ______________ of measurements and tolerances
calculate the costs	hand in the __________ of the costs
rehearse a presentation twice	make two ______________
know how to succeed	know the secret of ______________

Time for a smile

"Have you ever sold one of your paintings?"
"No," the artist replied, "but I'm encouraged. Somebody stole one."

TASK 4: Got a feeling for language?

There are five words for German "Fehler": **mistake, error, blunder, fault, defect.**
Which fits which sentence best?

1. Tom broke the window, but it was my ____________ for letting him play football in the house.
2. A hospital ____________ led to 500 cancer patients getting the wrong radiation treatment.
3. The causes of many birth ____________ have not yet been discovered.
4. I think there are a few ____________ in your calculations.
5. I accepted my father's ____________ because I loved him.
6. The letter had quite a few ____________ in it.

The Communicator's Corner

Overcoming objections

When negotiations between manufacturer and supplier, salesman and customer fail, it is because they cannot agree on one or more of the following issues:

The ten most common objections

1. service
2. reliability
3. availability, choice
4. continuity of supply
5. delivery
6. price
7. quality
8. guarantee
9. design
10. colour of product

Ten steps to overcome these objections

1. Be prepared. Anticipate concerns. Have a solution ready before the customer raises an objection.
2. If you haven't talked about customer benefits, shelve it: "Can I come back to that later?"
3. Don't interrupt. Listen patiently.
4. Pause and look thoughtful as if you're giving careful consideration to his or her objection. You gain more thinking time.
5. Feed the objection back to the customer.
   "So you think it costs too much. Today most things do, don't they."
6. Find out if the objection is a priority.
   "Can you tell me how much too much you think it is?"
   "So your hesitation is just this £300, isn't it?"
   Price is not a priority if the customer wants the product.
7. Ask whether the customer has other objections before you answer them one by one.
8. Use the FEEL-FELT-FOUND ANSWER.
   "I understand how you *feel* ... By the way, other clients also *felt* that ... then they *found* that they received good value for money from that product for about five years."
9. Counterbalance concerns with benefits.
10. Ask the closing "If-question".
    "If I can satisfy you regarding the price (delivery etc.), would you be ready to place an order?"

Witty quotes

An antique is something that's been useless so long that it's still in pretty good condition.
Franklin P. Jones

Art for art's sake makes no more sense than gin for gin's sake.
Somerset Maugham

Phrases for negotiators – Landing a contract

1. *Kundenvorteile ansprechen* – Talking about benefits

Wir haben genau die Produkte, die Ihren Anforderungen entsprechen.	We got just the products which can meet your requirements.
Ich bin absolut sicher, dass wir in diesem Punkt Ihren Bedarf decken können.	I'm absolutely certain we can cover your needs on that point.
Unser System hat drei wichtige Vorteile gegenüber der Konkurrenz.	Our system has three main advantages over our competitors.
Unser System ist Testsieger auf dem britischen Markt.	Our system has been rated best on the British market.

2. *Über Preise sprechen* – Discussing prices

Lassen Sie mich zuerst sagen, was Sie bekommen, dann können wir über den Preis reden.	Let me first tell you what you'll be getting, then we can talk about the price.
Der Preis ist offensichtlich sehr wichtig für Sie.	Price is obviously important for you.
Ist der Preis die einzige Entscheidungsgrundlage?	Is price your only consideration?
Wenn der Preis stimmt, kommen wir dann ins Geschäft?	So if the price is right, can we do business together?

TASK 5: What is the business verb?

1. __________ a customer's requirements
2. __________ customer needs
3. be __________ best by a consumer magazine
4. __________ business together

3. *Kompromiss schließen* – Striking a compromise

Ich bin sicher, wir kommen zu einer Einigung.	I'm sure we can come to an agreement on that.
Ich bin sicher, wir finden einen Kompromiss.	I'm sure we could find a way to strike a compromise.
Wir wollen Ihnen auf halbem Wege entgegenkommen.	We are ready to meet you half-way.
Wir sind bereit, gewisse Zugeständnisse zu machen.	We are prepared to make certain concessions.

4. *Bedingungen stellen* – Making stipulations

Wir wären bereit zu unterschreiben, vorausgesetzt, dass ...	We would be ready to sign, provided that ...
Wir wären bereit, Ihr Angebot zu akzeptieren, vorausgesetzt, dass ...	We would be willing to accept your offer, providing ...
Ich denke, wir könnten Ihrem Vorschlag zustimmen, unter der Bedingung, dass ...	I think we could agree to your suggestion on condition that ...
Wir sind bereit zu ... unter dem Vorbehalt, dass ...	We are willing to ... with the provision that ...

TASK 6: More business verbs to remember

1. __________ to an agreement
2. __________ a compromise
3. __________ someone halfway
4. __________ certain concessions
5. __________ an offer
6. __________ to a suggestion

The Psychologist's corner

The psychological tricks of professional negotiators

1. Make them like you!

They must like and trust you. This is the number-one psychological rule that decides if people will take a decision in your favour. Try to meet them on common ground, remind them of experiences they share with you, let them know that you respect them.

2. Narrow their options!

If you want people to do something don't give them more than three alternatives. The greater the choice, the less likely it is that they won't choose any of them. Fewer choices mean that they will make a decision faster.

3. Set them a deadline!

They will take longer to make a decision the more time you give them. The world operates on deadlines. It is human nature to wait if there is no need to act immediately. Let them know that your offer must be taken now because they won't get a second chance.

4. Sharpen their appetite!

We desire what is rare, what we cannot have or do. If you tell them that they may not get the opportunity to act in the future, you create a larger incentive to take a decision now. That is the reason why some shops put "sold" tags on items that they want to get rid of. When we see a "sold" tag on something we are unconsciously driven to desire it more.

5. Use the salami tactic!

Make them take small steps, ask them to take the large step at the end. If they agree to small requests the probability that they agree to larger requests later is infinitely greater.

6. Add the carrot!

Hold out the prospect of a little reward: "You may use this car for a week", "We'll go to dinner afterwards." The offer of any small additional benefit for taking action now will significantly increase your chances of getting a deal. The most incredible thing is that it almost doesn't matter what it is.

WORD AID

antique	*Antiquität*
assemble	*zusammenbauen*
availability	*Verfügbarkeit*
benefit	*Vorteil*
choice	*Wahl*
compensate	*Ersatz leisten*
concern	*Sorge*
counterbalance	*Gegenüberstellung, Gegengewicht*
deer	*Hirsch*
defective	*defekt, fehlerhaft*
flaw	*Fehler*
frame	*Rahmen*
hesitation	*Zögern*
incentive	*Anreiz*
incredible	*unglaublich*
issue	*Frage, Thema*
land a contract	*einen Abschluss an Land ziehen*
opponent	*Gegner*
part	*Teil; Bauteil*
proposal	*Vorschlag*
QC (quality control)	*Qualitätskontrolle*
raise an objection	*einen Einwand erheben*
range	*Baureihe*
rehearse	*proben*
request	*Bitte*
require	*erfordern, nötig machen*
responsive atmosphere	*positive, einladende Stimmung*
site; at the customer's ~	*beim Kunden, vor Ort*
supply	*liefern, versorgen*
tag	*Schild, Etikett*
tool	*Werkzeug*
win-win situation	*eine Situation, in der beide Seiten etwas gewinnen*

COMMUNICATING THROUGH ADS

Module 16

TIDYING UP THE EDGES

As we have seen in our journey through Busoom, communication is the transferring of what we want to say to somebody by some means or another. This means can be the written or spoken word, and can take place in various situations, for example, through presentations, meetings, counselling and interviews. In writing this occurs through letters, e-mails, reports etc. and, of course, by means of advertising. When the company creates its advertising, it wants to get across the company's special message or image to potential customers. That's part of communication and it's not so easy as we see at Busoom, but do not fear, Hardman's here!

We focus on

- the principles of advertising
- motivational research

Tidying up the edges

Hardman commissioned a small advertising agency, Image-maker, to create a quarter page advert in a trade journal. He is sitting together with Mr Fudge, the account manager from Image-maker. Hardman is definitely not amused.

H: Just look at this design and the wording! I'm sorry to sound so angry but this is really not what we wanted. (*This is what Hardman was reading*)

> **Why Buy Busoom's?**
> Our revolving doors are everything you've ever wanted,
> We have tried to integrate the latest technology,
> Whether you purchase the Smoothy, the Deluxe, or the Hardy,
> You will experience what it means to have quality and reliability.
> We are leaders in technology and have supplied industry for many years.

H: Well, it's wishy-washy and weak.

F: I don't know what you mean. Can you give me a pointer to what you don't like?

H: I certainly can. The sentences are long and spongy, nothing is put in a nutshell, no catchy phrase coined for Busoom.

F: It tells the truth about Busoom products, doesn't it?

H: My dear fellow, telling the truth to the world is fine, but we need much more. We need to show potential customers "why Busoom?" And I shouldn't be teaching you your job, should I? ... (*fade out*) (*Later Hardman is discussing his own proposals with Seaweed*)

H: Well, just look at this. The information is okay, but the packaging is lousy. Can we look at each line? "Buy at Busoom". We sound like a supermarket. I hope we're more upmarket than that. "A decision for Busoom", or better still "Your decision for Busoom". "Leading edge technology in revolving doors".

S: Yes, "we've tried to integrate ..." gives the impression that we haven't succeeded in integrating.

H: Quite! Next! "Customised design to your needs! – the Smoothy, the Deluxe, the Hardy!"

S: And we could finish with "Reliability, Quality and Know-how for industry".

H: Exactly! Now that's an example of operational excellence.

Your decision for Busoom,
Leading edge technology in revolving doors
Customised design to your needs
The Smoothy – the Deluxe – the Hardy!
Reliability, Quality and Know-how for industry

❖❖❖

And so we see that the first thing in advertising is to identify our target group. We have to be absolutely clear in our heads what our message is and finally in some way we must craft the form of the message. Indeed this is true of all communication, isn't it?

The Analyst's Corner

TASK 1: What's your comment?

1. What is basically wrong with Fudge's advert?
2. What fundamental improvements does Hardman make?
3. Can you comment on the structure of Hardman's advert?

Advice from the Experts

Doing business without advertising is throwing kisses to a lovely girl in the dark: you know what you are doing, but she doesn't.
Edgar Watson Howe

Advertising that uses superlatives isn't.
Harry Pesin

Advertising may be described as the science of arresting the human intelligence long enough to get money from it.
Stephen Leacock

WORKING with the language

TASK 2: Business phrases to remember

eine Agentur beauftragen	________ an agency
die neueste Technologie integrieren	integrate the ________ technology
in der Technologie führend sein	be __________ in technology
Wir sind anspruchsvoller.	We're more __________.
die Zielgruppe ausmachen	identify the __________ group
potenzielle Kunden erreichen	_____ _____ to potential customers
einen großen technologischen Vorsprung haben	have a leading __________ technology

TASK 3: Increase your word power

Find the verbs.

noun	verb
advertisement	__________
success	__________
purchase	__________
decision	__________

TASK 4: Idiomatic English

kurz gesagt, in einem Wort	to put it in a __________
jemandem einen Hinweis geben	give someone a __________
etwas den letzten Schliff geben	tidy up the __________

TASK 5: Preparing our psychologist's corner

Pair them off!
Which of the words in italics is explained by which definition?

1. *appeal* to basic instincts
2. show the product *benefits*
3. *target* the prospective customers
4. *trigger* an action
5. *convey* an idea

A. be of advantage or use to someone
B. be attractive or interesting to someone
C. transmit something
D. aim at someone
E. be the cause of / start something

Advice from the expert

All successful advertising campaigns which target men include one of these two messages:

A. This product will help you to get dates with bikini models.
B. This product will save you time and money, which you'll need if you want to date bikini models.

Your advertising message must appeal to women's greater range of intellectual interests and aesthetic preferences. Specifically, your message has to say this:

C. If you buy this product, you'll look like a bikini model.

Scott Adams, The Dilbert Principle

The Psychologist's corner

The Principles of Advertising

In advertising as in everything there are effective methods and not so effective methods. Take the following pairs of slogans for an electric shaver. Which one of each pair is the more effective? And why?

Slogan A	Slogan B
Shave effectively shave electrically	Why not shave in bed!

Well, the second is unusual and therefore attracts our attention. Furthermore, it conveys the idea of free time, of peace and quiet, it appeals to our laziness. That is what advertising is all about: attract attention, sell or suggest an idea, appeal to basic instincts like freedom, hope, fear and sex, show the product benefits and motivate the customer to make a buying decision. But what does it mean to appeal to instincts or to sell the idea of an article? Let's take a few examples:

Your product is ...	but you sell these ideas and feelings:
food	health, tasty meals, happy family
clothes	good looks, sexiness, class, image, power
shampoos	youthfulness , success with the opposite sex

Clever advertisers encapsulated their wisdom in the AIDA principle:

A attract people's **Attention**
I arouse their **Interest**, sell **Ideas**, appeal to **Instincts**
D help them to make a buying **Decision**
A motivate them to take **Action** and buy

The triggers of action

Of course it is all not as easy as it sounds. First, you have to do a market study, target the prospective customers. Then you have to learn how to arouse their interest, what instincts to appeal to and how to trigger an action. This is the field of the motivational researcher.

Do you know why you buy a certain shampoo? You do it, because some "triggers of action" make you buy the product. They can trigger off a buying decision on three different levels of human consciousness:
The first level is the conscious, rational level, where you know what is going on. You are able to tell me why you buy a certain brand of shampoo. This is the informative part of an ad. You buy it because it is the right product at the right time at the right price, not to forget the quality of your product and the service they offer you.

The second lower level is the preconscious level. You may know in a vague way what is going on within your own feelings and attitudes, but you would not be willing to tell anybody why you bought this shampoo. This is the level of prejudices, hopes and fears.

The third level is where you are not only not aware of your motives for buying the shampoo, but would not discuss them if you could.

Exploring your attitudes towards your shampoo on the second and third level has become MR (motivational research), a new science. The aim of MR is to manipulate your motivations and desires in such a way that you develop a need for that shampoo which you didn't have before.

Time for a smile

He went to the newspaper office to put an ad in the paper offering $5,000 reward for the return of his wife's cat. The man behind the counter said: "That's a lot of reward, isn't it?" He replied, "it doesn't matter. I drowned the damned cat."

WORD AID

account manager	*Kundenbetreuer*
attitude	*Einstellung, Haltung*
benefit	*Vorteil, Nutzen*
catchy phrases	*schmissige Sätze*
commission	*in Auftrag geben*
conscious	*bewusst*
consciousness	*Bewusstsein*
convey an idea	*eine Idee vermitteln / transportieren*
craft the form of a message	*eine Botschaft sorgfältig formulieren*
customised design	*maßgeschneidertes Design*
date	*Verabredung, Rendezvous*
drown	*ertränken*
edge	*Schneide; Vorteil; Vorsprung*
look round	*sich umdrehen; rundlich aussehen*
means; by ~ of	*mittels, durch*
occur	*geschehen; vorkommen, passieren*
pointer, give someone a ~	*jemandem einen Hinweis geben*
preconscious	*vorbewusst*
preference	*Vorliebe*
prejudice	*Vorurteil*
purchase	*(ein)kaufen*
reliability	*Zuverlässigkeit*
reward	*Belohnung*
shaver	*Rasierapparat*
slim	*schlank*
spongy	*schwammig*
succeed in	*Erfolg haben bei*
trigger	*Auslöser; auslösen*
upmarket; be ~	*exklusiver, anspruchsvoller sein*
wording	*Formulierung*

Sign in a shop window

Our clothes not only make girls slim,
they also make men look round.

DEALING WITH FOREIGNERS

Module 17

THE AMERICAN WAY

Throughout the book we have come into contact with various problems of communication and their solutions. To make matters worse in addition to all these normal communication issues, there is an extra factor – the foreigner. These are people from a different environment. Their expressions, their language and attitudes are all different from ours. This complicates matters. Everything becomes even more difficult when we remember that there are many sorts of foreigners each with their own types of behaviour. We can't go into all those things here. Our "snapshot" will be limited to Busoom's visitor, Mr Grabit, from the USA.

We focus on

- cultural differences between Americans and Germans
- national stereotypes
- the American manager
- and some differences between British and American English

The American way

Mr Hirsch (**H**), the new marketing director from Berlin, has a meeting with Mr Grabit (**G**) from Do-A-Door in the States. The idea is to introduce and sell a line of doors to the USA.

H: (*fade in*) ... so I really enjoyed myself in California just taking it easy. They were four great weeks in my life[1].

G: I bet they were. Four weeks![2] Anyhow, time is money. Let's get down to it, shall we? You want to sell your doors back in the States. Well, how many doors at what price can you offer us? Inter-company, of course[3].

H: Well, but first of all I'd like to explain the results of our research to you, which I believe is rather extensive[4].

G: Well, what's the bottom line?

H: So first of all I want to show you the results of our survey. What we did was to send questionnaires to ... (*fade out*)

G: (*fade in*)That's all well and good, Mr Hirsch, but if we could come to the point, what's the bottom line?

H: What do you mean "bottom line?"

G: It's as clear as clear can be. How many doors, how many customers and what's the profit?[5]

H: Okay, if you look at this third spreadsheet you'll see that in total in the first quarter we'd sell more than 3,000 systems on this forecast.

G: Now you're talking figures. Now we're really making progress. 3,000, now that means[6] ... (*fade out*)

H: (*fade in*) ... we've calculated the costs of manufacturing the door systems for the American market. As you probably realise it'll be necessary to set up a small production unit in New England. I ...

G: (*interrupting*) What the devil for? We want to make money, not reduce unemployment[7].

H: I'm sorry. I don't quite follow you.

---

1 Please note, that the numbers in the text refer to our comments on the typical behaviour of the German and the American manager in this meeting.

G: It's crystal clear! We don't want overheads. So we don't want staff. Everything should be done by sub-contracting, so we can protect ourselves and keep our costs down[8].

H: But what about quality assurance in that case?

G: Oh, my God! ...

WORKING with the language

TASK 1: Business phrases to remember

zur Sache kommen	come to the ________
die Ergebnisse der Forschung	the results of the ________
die Ergebnisse einer Umfrage	the findings of a ________
eine Produktionsstätte einrichten	____ ___ a small production unit
die Arbeitslosigkeit verringern	________ unemployment
die Kosten niedrig halten	________ costs ____
Wir wollen keine Fixkosten.	We don't want ________.
Fortschritte machen	make ________

Time for a smile

And there was this good-looking East-Friesian who went surfriding.

His horse drowned.

The Analyst's Corner

The numbers here refer to the numbers in the dialogue.

1. Hirsch thinks he is paying America and Mr Grabit a compliment. He is trying to build bridges, to find common ground and set up a good atmosphere. It went down wrong with Grabit.
2. Employees in the States get far fewer holidays. Not a good start. Grabit probably thinks Hirsch is a time-waster. His reaction might be "envy" or disbelief. Already a cultural problem.
3. Our American friend wants the bottom line. Figures and profits. This does not satisfy his German counterpart.
4. Germans generally want to have all the relevant details before reaching any agreement. They plod through fact by fact, line by line. This can be extremely frustrating for their partners in business.
5. Whereas the German businessman or engineer needs his details, even too much detail, his partner from the US wants an overall picture without any detail. The other extreme.
6. Americans are interested in results. Now Grabit really thinks that progress has been made, he feels at home with figures and forecasts.
7. American businessmen can be direct, bordering on rude. So can the German businessman, but he has more of a feeling of following the rules of politeness.
8. Here we have another difference in mentality. The German prefers to build something solid, reliable and to do it slowly, whereas our US friends like to buy knowledge and services as cheaply and quickly as possible.

Time for a smile

An Englishman was boasting that some of his ancestors had been in the ark with Noah. "At the time of the flood," retorted the Scot, "we, the MacGregrors, had our own boat."

Cultural differences – how they listen, what they expect

Meetings the American way	Meetings the German way
Americans are good listeners when subjects interest them	Germans (and Swedes) are the best listeners of all nations
attention span: 30 minutes	attention span: 1 hour or more
they expect catch phrases and hard sell	they expect lots of prints, figures, delivery dates etc.
they listen to be entertained	they listen for information, ask questions to make sure they have understood correctly
they want to be sold the product	they are interested in the price
they expect modernity, they want the short-term deal rather than a long-term relationship	they expect solidity of the company and solidity of the product; they are interested in business partnership

TASK 2: What do they understand by truth?

For Germans and Americans the way to successful contracts is keeping to the truth, keeping one's word. This not always the case with other nations. Even our closest neighbours see it differently. Can you match these statements against the following nations?

	Nation		Attitude towards truth
1	Italy, France	A	there is no absolute truth
2	Britain	B	adherence to the truth must not destroy the balance of society
3	Japan	C	the truth is the truth as long it doesn't rock the boat (create unnecessary problems)
4	China	D	smooth social relationships are more important than the truth

TASK 3: Understanding the Americans

Can you match American against British English?

American English		British English	
1.	You're the CEO.	A	Accountants can be frustrating.
2.	Sure!	B	What do you think of that?
3.	How does that grab you?	C	I'm not quite with you on that.
4.	Bean-counters drive me mad.	D	I'm afraid, we all have to do our homework first.
5.	You're talking bullshit.	E	How interesting, however ...
6.	Jack'll blow his top.	F	We've some fine products to offer to you.
7.	You gotta be kidding!	G	You are the managing director.
8.	Got some goodies for you.	H	Of course!
9.	I tell you, I can walk away from this deal.	I	Our chairman might disagree.

TASK 4: Cultural awareness test

Nations differ as to the way they conduct meetings and presentations. Hirsch and Grabit would have got along much better with each other if they had known about these cultural differences. What about you? Mark the American way with an **A**, the German way with a **G** and learn about yourself.

	Meetings the American way (A) and the German way (B)	A or G?	
1.	They start with humour, jokes, wisecracks.		
2.	They start with introductions and the agenda; no jokes.		
3.	They expect to be addressed with their titles.		
4.	Their meetings have a beginning, a middle and an end; one thing at a time, step by step.		
5.	They are quickly on first-name terms at the first meeting.		
6.	They want you to put your cards on the table at once; no beating around the bush.		

7.	Communication is explaining, asking questions, exchanging and testing views.		
8.	Communication is a fight: they confront, provoke, they use sarcasm and kidding.		
9.	They listen to an argument and reply with a counter-argument.		
10.	They make an offer and expect a counter-offer.		
11.	They want 'Yes' in principle; details can be settled later.		
12.	They want to settle the details first and then take a decision.		
13.	Everybody should come well-prepared. No surprises, no spontaneous presentations.		
14.	They tend to start with presentations that listeners are not always prepared for.		
15.	They expect clarity, reliability. They need time to deliberate and test the offers.		
16.	They seek the instant deal; they wish to do the business as soon as possible.		

TASK 5: How good a guest would you be?

Are these statements true (T) or false (F)? **T / F**

1.	If you are invited to an American home, you should bring flowers for the hostess.		
2.	Americans normally wish each other "Good appetite" before they begin a meal together.		
3.	It is considered polite to leave a little bit of food on your plate when you have finished eating.		
4.	Guests usually offer to help in the kitchen.		
5.	If you need to go to the toilet ask "May I use your toilet, please?"		
6.	When they ask you "How do you like the USA?" they expect you to give a frank and honest answer.		
7.	If you feel hot, you may ask if you can open a door or a window, although almost all rooms are air-conditioned.		

TASK 6: Would you know what you get to eat there?

Here are two lists with English and American snacks.
Can you match them off?

	American English		British English
1	French fries	A	steak and lobster
2	cookie	B	crisps
3	biscuit	C	biscuit
4	surf-and-turf	D	scone
5	potato chips	E	chips

Time for a smile

The American tourist was visiting a zoo in London. In front of the kangaroo house he stopped dead, still chewing. Said he, "One thing I really grant you, Brits. Your grass-hoppers are really a lot bigger than ours back in Texas."

National Stereotypes or How Europeans see each other

The human brain loves to generalise, that is why we cannot resist generalising about national characters although we know that 90 percent of the Italians are not good lovers, that not all Englishmen are cold-blooded and that most Americans are not as blunt as John Wayne.

A market research firm, the Parkland Research Europe, carried out an opinion poll among 185 business executives, lawyers, engineers, teachers and other professional people from seven European countries. They published their findings in the *Guide to National Practices in Western Europe*. Here is a summary of what other nations thought of the Germans and the British.

Let us take the British first. The reactions were mixed. Some found them calm, stiff, reserved, open-minded and trustworthy. Others think they are hidebound and superior. Everyone was unanimous that they had an excellent sense of good humour. The British themselves most admired the characters of the Dutch.

What about the Germans? Most Europeans agreed that the Germans had a high proportion of good qualities. And the Germans, of course, liked themselves best of all nations. They considered themselves tolerant, but nobody else did. They saw themselves as fashionable. Others found them square. The Italians are dumbfounded by the German capacity to get things done without bribing anyone, but regard them as utterly lacking in style. The French regard the Germans with suspicion and a measure of loathing, and seek to contain them by chumming-up. To the Austrians a good German would be one who is far away – preferably across the Atlantic, or even further if they didn't depend on the deutschmarks of the German tourists that prevents their economy from collapsing. The English have always had a high regard for German cleverness and thoroughness, somehow imagining that of all Europeans, the Germans are most like themselves. This illusion probably has its roots in the fact that so many Germans have occupied the British throne or been powers behind it.

The Germans regard the English as being very nice and mostly harmless, almost German. They respect the Swiss for their seriousness, honesty, punctuality and cleanliness – and they have never been to war with the Swiss. However, they like the Americans best. For the Germans, the United States is the headmaster in the school of nations.

Adapted from S. Zeidenitz, B. Barkow, *The Xenophobe's Guide to The Germans.*

Here are a few selected national stereotypes

As soon as the German tourist gets to Paradise,
he will ask for picture postcards.

❖ ❖ ❖

One German makes a philosopher,
two a public meeting,
three a war.

Robert MacDonald, *Summit Conference*, 1982

Why do Germans envy the Chinese?
Because they have still got their Wall.

The following joke, which probably originated at a conference of journalists, pokes fun at various national faiblesses – French lust, German seriousness, American bragging, British colonialism etc.

English:	Hunting elephants in British East Africa.
French:	The love life of elephants in French Equatorial Africa.
German:	The origin and development of the East African elephant in the years 1200 – 1950 (600 pages).
American:	How to breed bigger and better elephants.
Russian:	How we sent an elephant to the moon.
Swede:	Elephants and the welfare state.
Dane:	Elephant-meat and smørrebrød.

Richard D. Lewis, *When Cultures Collide. Managing successfully across cultures.* London 1996

The American Manager

With regard to their employees many American bosses see themselves in the role of a coach rather than a boss. However, there is a well-defined distance between both. Beneath the relaxed and familiar style and the ready use of first names, there is a strict code of manners. Like in football the American coach gives more directions than advice. Both, bosses and coaches manage and direct their teams during the course of a competition.

American bosses have not the reputation of being skilled or patient in dealing with arguments from their subordinates. Discussions are open to the point of being brusque. They tend to see disagreement as insubordination rather than constructive criticism. As Samuel Goldwyn once said: "I don't want any yes-men around me. I want everybody to tell me the truth – even if it costs them their jobs."

Time is money. The American is always on the go, always in a hurry, rarely stopping to enjoy the present – a slave to the clock. That is why he (or she) had to invent fast food and instant coffee. He treats time as a valuable and limited resource. Like money he saves it, wastes it, gives it, takes it, spends it, runs out of it and budgets it.

This affects his way of conducting business. He often lacks patience and will say provocative things to get things moving. Whether it is a job interview, sales call, or any other kind of business meeting, the American will be on time. To arrive early, however, would suggest that the visitor has time to spare, an impression one would wish to avoid.

American managers have difficulties in adapting to business cultures where time is flexible, where drinking coffee and chatting is considered as doing something and not as a waste of time.

Adapted from Copeland & Griggs, *Going International*

Time for a smile

An American CEO on his trip to Europe on a Concorde was busy studying the ways and traditions of the European countries he was going to visit. As they were flying over Europe, the stewardess, in an attempt to make the trip entertaining, said. "That's Paris down there, sir."

"Don't bother me with details," snapped the executive. "Just mention the continents."

WORD AID

accountant	*Buchhalter*
addition; in ~ to	*zusätzlich zu*
adherence to the truth	*Wahrheitstreue*
advice	*Rat*
affect	*beeinflussen, beeinträchtigen*
agenda	*Tagesordnung*
ark	*Arche*
assurance	*Versicherung*
attention span	*Aufmerksamkeitspanne*
beat around the bush	*wie die Katze um den heißen Brei herumgehen, um die Sache herumreden*
blunt	*ungeschliffen, derb, ungehobelt*
bluntness	*schonungslose Offenheit*
boast	*prahlen*
bottom line; what's the ~ ~	*wie sieht es unter dem Strich aus?, worauf läuft es hinaus?*
bribe	*bestechen*
chum up with someone	*sich mit jemandem anfreunden*
contain someone	*im Zaum halten*
contract	*Vertrag*
depend on	*abhängig sein von*
development	*Entwicklung*
directions	*Anweisungen*
dumbfounded	*verblüfft, sprachlos*
extensive	*umfangreich*
fashionable	*modisch, modebewusst*
findings	*Ergebnisse*
forecast	*Vorhersage, Schätzung*
foreigner	*Ausländer*
generalise	*verallgemeinern*
hidebound	*engstirnig, beschränkt, borniert*

hostess	*Gastgeberin*
instant deal	*schneller Abschluss*
insubordination	*Ungehorsam*
inter-company	*von Firma zu Firma*
opinion poll	*Meinungsumfrage*
origin	*Ursprung*
overheads	*Gemeinkosten*
prevent from	*hindern an*
provoke	*provozieren*
questionnaire	*Fragebogen*
reliability	*Zuverlässigkeit*
research	*Forschung*
retort	*erwidern*
rock the boat	*die Sache gefährden*
scone	*weiches Teegebäck*
smooth	*glatt, sanft, reibungsfrei*
spreadsheet	*elektronisches Arbeitsblatt; Tabellenkalkulation*
square	*anständig, ehrlich*
staff	*Personal*
subordinate	*Untergebener*
suggest	*vorschlagen, nahe legen*
superior	*überlegen, überheblich; Vorgesetzter*
survey	*Umfrage, Gutachten, Bericht*
thoroughness	*Gründlichkeit*
unanimous	*einstimmig*
valuable	*wertvoll*
view	*Ansicht, Meinung*
welfare state	*Wohlfahrtsstaat*
wisecrack	*treffende Bemerkung; Witzelei*
worse; to make matters ~	*was die Angelegenheit noch verschlimmert*

EPILOGUE

HARDMAN'S QUIZ

During the last seventeen modules we've been taking a bird's eye view of some of the communication issues of Busoom Ltd. You will have noticed, Dear Reader, that like every other company they suffered with their correspondence, one-to-one connections, wishy-washy, inefficient meetings, telephone behaviour and small-talking in general.

On the credit side Busoom was lucky enough to have a management that was forward-looking and aggressive enough to tackle all these issues to change the direction of communication in their company. The ship's captain, Mr Hardman, is a very experienced and dynamic leader who knows where he wants to go. As you will have observed his key-phrase in business life is "operational excellence". This means that tasks must be seen to be performed as optimally as possible so that time and money are not wasted and so that other people's time and work is not disturbed.
During this year Hardman worked consistently on improving channels of communication through discipline, discussion and training. And so it was that on June 2, Hardman's birthday, Mrs Velvet, his assistant came running into Hardman's office. "Could you come into the conference room as quickly as possible? There's been an accident or something with Mr Seaweed."

Hardman and Velvet ran into the room through the automatic slider to be greeted by a chorus of happy birthday, dear Big Boss, happy birthday to you! Seaweed makes a mini-speech which suits him well. "We want to thank you for trying to save this sinking ship. We appreciate your efforts and we all believe we're on the right track."

Hardman needed a few seconds to recover from his surprise before he was able to reply.
"Thank you all so much. I also feel we're on the way. And by the way, when I look around me and see all these wonderful cakes and even alcohol which is, of course, not allowed at Busoom any more, I can only say that this is real Busoom operational excellence at its best. Thank you, my friends. Oh, by the way, since we're all here together, would you do me a little favour and do this little quiz while you finish your drinks?"

Hardman's quiz

1. At work you have a very pleasant, friendly colleague. Unfortunately, she insists on coming to talk to you about private matters, especially when you're under time pressure. You don't want to upset her. Should you
   A. drop hints and hope she gets the message,
   B. tell her politely that you've got no time but you'll talk to her later,
   C. ignore her and carry on with your work?

2. You have arranged a meeting with a supplier to finalise an order which you've already cleared with your colleagues. The supplier arrives, but your boss joins the meeting and puts the whole arrangement into question and doubts the supplier is the right man for the job. Should you
   A. sit back and let the supplier battle it out,
   B. take your boss aside and tell him he is out of order,
   C. cancel the meeting with an apology to the supplier, until you and your team are better prepared?

3. You attend a meeting with a customer and find him drunk and aggressive. Do you
   A. draw attention to his condition and complain about it, then leave,
   B. try to humour him and leave on good terms,
   C. invent an excuse and leave immediately?

4. By chance you find out that two married colleagues are having a love affair. Do you
   - A. do nothing and hope everything will take care of itself,
   - B. report the affair to your boss and leave it to him,
   - C. confront the two lovers and tell them be reasonable?

5. You are informed that your company is about to stop using a supplier with whom you have a good relationship. You know this will be dangerous for the business. What do you do?
   - A. Nothing, but prepare yourself to explain the action when he is informed,
   - B. try to persuade your colleagues to allow you to give the supplier early warning of the decision,
   - C. tell the supplier personally and confidentially?

6. One of your colleagues treats a business contact rudely in a meeting that you're attending. You feel that you are also co-responsible for this. Should you
   - A. apologise to the contact on behalf of your colleague,
   - B. ask your colleague's boss to make him apologise,
   - C. make a friendly call to your contact to make sure he knows you're not the same rude type as your colleague?

7. You hear that a good customer of yours is being investigated by the police on a charge of shoplifting. Next time you speak to him should you
   - A. mention you've heard about it and wish him luck,
   - B. wait for him to mention it,
   - C. offer your support to him with actually mentioning the specific case?

8. A customer is very dissatisfied. A meeting with him is so bad that he threatens physical violence. Should you
   - A. reciprocate the threat,
   - B. warn him how serious his threat is and call for witnesses,
   - C. leave as quickly as possible?

9. You're at a meeting with your boss. He very often gets facts wrong and draws wrong conclusions. Should you

A. let it go and have a word with him afterwards,

B. politely interrupt to put matters right,

C. find an excuse to take your colleague to one side to point out his mistakes?

10. You have joined a company and find out that you are expected to socialise outside office hours. You are a shy person. What should you do?

A. Pretend to be more social that you are,

B. do the minimum to seem sociable,

C. avoid joining in?

Adapted from *Business Etiquette*, David Robinson

WORD AID

WORD AID

bird's eye view	*Überblick*
apology	*Entschuldigung*
behaviour	*Verhalten*
complain	*sich beschweren*
consistently	*beständig, konstant, unbeirrbar*
disturb	*stören*
doubt	*(be)zweifeln*
finalise an order	*eine Bestellung abschließen*
insist on	*bestehen auf*
interrupt	*unterbrechen*
recover	*sich erholen*
shoplifting	*Ladendiebstahl*
slider	*Schiebetür*
sociable	*gesellig*
suit someone well	*jemandem gut stehen / passen*
tackle an issue	*ein Problem anpacken*
threat	*Drohung*
track	*Spur, Weg*
upset someone	*jemanden aus der Fassung bringen*
violence	*Gewalt*
witness	*Zeuge*

KEY TO THE EXERCISES

MODULE 1

TASK 1: Business phrases to remember

we'll *get back to* you	we'll be in *touch with* you
the results are *important*	it's results that *count*
let's *try and solve* the problem	let's *tackle* the problem
he didn't *get* the job	he didn't *land* the job
a subsidiary belongs to *it*	a subsidiary belongs to a *parent company*

TASK 2: First words

Good morning. *How are* you?	*Fine*, thank you.
Nice to *see* you.	It's *good* to *meet* you.
Pleased to meet you.	The *pleasure* is mine.

TASK 3: Streamlining Lost's language

There *were quite a few* things to do in our department ...	I *identified* problems in our department ...
... and I *got over* the problems *easily enough*.	... and I *suggested* solutions that *solved* our problems once and for all.
I *handled* the *advertising* for ...	I *mounted* a successful advertising *campaign* for ...
I *helped to market* our new X15.	I *launched* our new X 15 and *increased* its profitability.
I *was involved* in personnel training.	I *successfully* trained staff.
I *was given* a *task* ...	I *achieved* my targets to the fullest *satisfaction* of my superiors.

TASK 4: Increase your word power

1. Four expressions the German *Ziel*: target, aim, goal, objective
2. Three synonyms for *mean*: show, signal, convey
3. Three words for *nachmachen*: imitate, match, mirror

TASK 5: Communication quiz

Communication needs are communication styles

Typical male needs:	Typical female needs:
1. to feel accepted	2. to feel respected
3. to feel admired	4. to feel understood
5. to feel appreciated	6. to feel reassured
7. to feel approved of	8. to feel cared about
10. to feel validated	9. to feel trusted

MODULE 2

TASK 1: Sit back and think

1. Hardman is annoyed that he has no flipchart for his meeting. As we see from Seaweed's comment later Hardman had been informed. He could have avoided the problem by listening more carefully.
   Excuse: The meeting was loud.
   Advice: Listen to people, slow down, take a minute to register what they say, turn and face them. No shouting!
2. Dr Geisel didn't stop to think, to listen. He has already confused the issue. He missed Hardman's words "reception desk". He was thinking of an entirely different door.
3. His behaviour is unprofessional because he allows emotion to come in. The other participants must try to eliminate the emotional context to get at what is fact and intent.
4. Hardman has become over-emotional. That's not effective. By this time he's not listening to anybody. He uses strong, negative language (robbers / blurbs).

5. Seaweed is more neutral. He is analysing the situation. He must exclude Hardman's emotion and check what is wanted by intelligent questioning and rephrasing.

TASK 2: Enlarge your business English

einen Überblick über die Themen geben	give an *overview* of the *items*
sich mit einem Problem / Kunden befassen	*deal with* a problem / a customer
auf eine Lösung warten	wait *for a solution*
aneinander vorbeireden	be talking *at cross*-purposes
Verschwendung wertvoller Zeit	*waste* of *valuable* time
nach dem Stand der Dinge fragen	ask *for* a *status* report
jemandes Bedürfnisse / Bedarf überprüfen	check someone's *needs*
in Betrieb sein	be in *operation*

TASK 3: Bits and pieces

1. Translate the German in brackets:
   We have dealt with three items *since* our last meeting.
   I've been waiting *for* weeks for a solution.
2. Remember the two words for *zufrieden*?
   How could they be *content*?
   Production were very *satisfied.*
3. Use an infinitive with *to*:
   I find the doors *to be* okay.
   There is no space *to write.*

TASK 4: Communication practice

I can imagine how you must feel.	6
Would you believe it?	3
Tell me more.	2
I wonder.	5
Definitely!	4
Incredible!	3
Well done!	1/4
How extraordinary!	2
You don't say so!	2/3
I can't blame you.	4
Really?	5
Good for you!	1
Who knows?	5
Of course!	4
I know what it's like.	6

TASK 5: Active listener's treasure chest

A.

Das ist erstaunlich.	It's *amazing.*
Unglaublich!	*Incredible! Unbelievable!*
Das ist einmalig / unerhört!	That *beats* everything!

B.

Erzählen Sie mir mehr davon.	Please, *tell* me *more.*
Das ist höchst interessant.	That's *most* interesting.
Tolle Geschichte!	*What* a story!

C.

Ich sehe das auch so.	I think *so, too.*
Ich verstehe, was Sie meinen.	I *see* your point.
Ich bin ganz Ihrer Meinung.	I absolutely *agree* with you.
Sie treffen den Nagel auf den Kopf.	You've *hit* the nail on the *head.*

D.

Sind Sie sicher? Ist das wirklich Ihr Ernst? Was Sie nicht sagen! Kaum zu glauben!	Are you *sure*? Do you really *mean* that? You don't *say*! Can you *believe* it?

MODULE 3

TASK 1: Sit back and think

1. Using body language, open, friendly positions, eye to eye contact is important. Facing your conversation partner. Giving a relaxed and welcoming feeling. And he involves Dump in the responsibility.
2. Seaweed repeats his topics of health being of great importance and a serious responsibility. With this repetition he wants to make his position clear to Dump.
3. Seaweed is concise and direct. He doesn't use jargon or talk with a lot of fancy words and expressions. KISS – keep it simple / stupid. His proposal or information is simple and direct.
4. It's a good idea to have your notepad and take down information. Your discussion partner feels that you are really interested in his position. He feels respected.
5. When you want to influence people, you need the right atmosphere. Make sure your mobile is switched off – if you have one, or that your telephone is switched to your secretary or somewhere else. This shows that you take your conversation partner seriously. It's no good being interrupted when everybody's deeply involved in serious issues.

TASK 2: Business phrases to remember

eine zehnminütige Zigarettenpause	a ten-minute *smoking break*
etwas akzeptieren, übernehmen	take something on *board*
mit dem Betriebsrat sprechen	talk to the *works council*
die Interessen der Arbeiter vertreten	*represent* the interests of the workers
besondere Regeln einführen	*introduce* special *rules*
für das Personal verantwortlich sein	be *responsible* for the *staff*
zur Sache kommen	come to the *point*
Ich wünsche keine weiteren Unterbrechungen.	I want no *further interruptions.*
alles so einfach wie möglich halten	*keep* everything *as* simple *as* possible
die Mehrheit unterstützen	*support* the majority

TASK 3: Rules about communication

1. *maintain* personal relationships, get your *message* across
2. the main *purpose* of your message
3. *receive* the message
4. be *simple*, keep to the main *subject*
5. *check* the facts
6. *strike* the right tone, *targeted at*

TASK 4: Compare and complete

On the phone	In writing
Do we get the goods cheaper if we buy more than 1000?	Would you *grant* us a *reduction* if we *purchase* in excess of 1000 items?
Can you let us have the goods by Tuesday?	Would it be possible *to deliver* the goods by Tuesday?
The goods were no good.	The goods were of *inferior* quality.
Sorry, but if you can't send us the goods on time we must find somebody else to get us the articles.	We *regret* to say that if it is impossible to keep the *deadline* we will be obliged to find an alternative *supplier.*

MODULE 4

TASK 1: Business phrases to remember

Ideen austauschen	*exchange* ideas
Angestellte einstellen	*take on* employees
die Vereinbarung lesen	read the *agreement*
zu einer Entscheidung / einem Schluss kommen	*come* to a conclusion
ein Seminar durchführen	*carry out* a seminar
ein Geschäft leiten	*run* a business
jemandes Botschaft verstehen	*get* someone's message

TASK 2: Food for thought

1. It's important in business (as in our private life) what our body language tells our conversation partner. By putting his hands on the table (spreading them), looking directly into Misfit's eyes, but not raising his voice or being somehow aggressive , Hardman is open and fair.
2. Avoiding eye contact can be a sign of nervousness and even untruthfulness. Of course it's also no good to stare for long periods into a person's eyes. This is a confrontative, aggressive act. Find the happy medium. In the dialogue Misfit gives Hardman the impression he may not be telling the truth. He rubs his nose, creating an impression of not being relaxed.
3. If a conversation partner "plays" with things, especially tearing up sheets of paper into small pieces, this is usually a sign that he is insecure.
4. As with paper-tearing, rubbing your hands shows that something is wrong. Insecurity and worry are conveyed by this action.
5. An important part of communication through body language is the body position – the posture. Sitting hunched up shows a beaten, insecure soul. Here Misfit knows what he is saying is not appropriate and possibly not true.

TASK 3: Interpreting body language

1. Tent	B. self confidence	Sicherheit
2. Prayer	C. anxiety	Angst
3. Nose touch	B. doubt	Zweifel
4. 'L' chin rest	D. evaluation	Abschätzung
5. Arms up	A. reservation	Zurückhaltun
6. Lean forward	B. readiness	Bereitschaft
7. Thumbs out	D. authority	Autorität

TASK 4: Balance the Magic Squares

A = 4	B = 9	C = 2
D = 3	E = 5	F = 7
G = 8	H = 1	I = 6

TASK 5: Words for defusing an angry customer

1. Listen and ask

Would you be so kind as to *describe* your problem?
I'll make a few *notes.*
I'm just *taking* this down.

2. Show sympathy

I *understand* your dissatisfaction.
I can imagine your *disappointment.*
I'm sure your complaint is *justified.*

3. Apologise even if you are right

I'm extremely sorry for any inconvenience this has *caused* you.
Please *accept* our apology.
I do *apologise* for the error made by our accounts department.

4. Finding solutions

What do you *expect* us to do in this case?
We'll of course *replace* the article.
Or would you *prefer* to have your money *back*?

5. Last words

I'm pleased we managed to *sort* it all out.
I'm relieved that we were able to *solve* your problem.
Don't *hesitate* to call again should another problem crop up.

MODULE 5

TASK 1: Business phrases to remember

Ziele zu hoch stecken	set *targets* too high
inclusive Versicherung	*including* insurance
Beschwerdebrief	letter of *complaint*
eine lehrreiche Erfahrung	a *learning* experience
seine Unzufriedenheit zum Ausdruck bringen	express one's *dissatisfaction*
eine Karte ist noch gültig	a card is still *valid*
jemandes Wünschen entsprechen	*comply* with someone's wishes
eine negative Auswirkung auf die Geschäftsbeziehung	a negative effect on the business *relationship*

TASK 2: Comparing the letters

The first letter

1. She did not communicate with the reader or recipient. For example, she didn't give a date so the reader doesn't know how current the complaint is.
2. She didn't use the company logo so the reader doesn't know the status of the writer.
3. The context was not logical point by point. We'll come back to that later.
4. The complimentary close was not appropriate (*Best wishes* is informal, *Yours sincerely* would be better) and the language was informal.

The second letter

1. It's good to have sections with underlined headlines to focus the reader's attention and to help him set priorities.
2. The complaints should be logically structured. Thus, first we should describe the historical background. This information should be given chronologically.

3. After the background information we should state the consequences. What were the negative results of all this? What might the financial implications be?
4. Action, commonly known as the threat. We will take action if you do not ...

TASK 3: Misty Card reacts

We were indeed very sorry to hear about the *inconvenience* you had using our Misty Card.
After a thorough analysis of your case we are happy to *assure* you that the disturbance was not caused by any *deficiency* inherent in your Misty Card, but due entirely to *circumstances* beyond our *control.* It seems that British Telecom lines sometimes fail to cope with demands at peak hours.
I *enclose* a cheque of £300 for the extra night you had to stay in Britain and very much *regret* the inconvenience the *inadequacy* of British computer lines has caused you. I also hope that this *incident* will not have a negative effect on our future business relationship and assure you that this will not occur in future.

TASK 4: The perfect letter

A. The first and the last line

1. A letter to a man you do not know: *Dear Sir* (no comma)
2. A letter to a lady you do not know: *Dear Madam*
3. You don't know if the recipient is male or female: *Dear Sir or Madam*
4. A letter to a company: *Dear Sirs*
5. You end the above letters with *Yours faithfully / Yours sincerely.*
6. You end a letter that starts with *Dear Mr Bossy* with *Yours sincerely.*
7. When do you start it like this: *Dear Mrs Henriette Hornsucker?* You don't!

B. The first or the last sentence of the main body?

	first	last
8. we hope you will appreciate our position		✗
9. we regret to have to tell you that	✗	

10.	we should like to remind you that	✗	
11.	we look forward to hearing from you		✗
12.	we wish to draw your attention to	✗	

C. What type of letter do the sentences belong to?

13. If you have already sent a remittance please disregard this letter.
A. a reminder

14. I would like to widen my experiences and to work in a field with more responsibility. **B.** an application

15. We thank your very much for your cooperation and guarantee you the strictest confidence. **B.** an enquiry

16. On the 14th June we placed an order for 120 electric motors, type M200 produced by you. **C.** a complaint

The magic squares

A = 2	B = 7	C = 6
D = 9	E = 5	F = 1
G = 4	H = 3	I = 8

MODULE 6

TASK 1: Business phrases to remember

vom Vorstand genehmigt	*approved* by the Board
Marktstudie in Auftrag geben	commission a *survey* of the market
Einführungspreise anbieten	offer *introductory* prices
das Thema wechseln	*change* the topic
ein Abkommen aushandeln	*negotiate a* supplier agreement
Marktführer für Türen	*market* leader for doors
Umsatzziele um 20 Prozent übertreffen	*exceed* sales *targets* by 20 percent
eine Produktreihe einführen	*launch* a product *range*

TASK 2: How do you see it?

1. The first part of real communication in interviewing is to take the time to read and digest the CV of the candidate. Many employers only seem to find time for it at the interview itself. By preparing Seaweed shows he takes the candidate seriously and can ask the right questions.
2. It is an example of direct communication skill: eye contact, friendly handshake. Seaweed stands up, takes trouble with his candidate. He communicates openness, friendliness and fairness.
3. Icebreakers: Seaweed asks about the travel and offers refreshments. He shows he wants to make Bono feel at home.
4. Seaweed shows he has read the CV and goes into detail. This communicates real interest and seriousness.
5. This type of question is absolutely relevant to the application. It helps to create an overall impression of the candidate. Questions which are irrelevant should be eliminated.
6. Seaweed is seeking common ground, common experience to link up psychologically to the candidate. This tactic will relax both of the people.

TASK 3: Do you know what a CV should look like?

	yes	no
The essential aim is to interest an employer so that he wants to know more about you.	✗	
Your CV must include your date of birth.	✗	
Mention evening classes and courses, even those you attended for personal reasons.		✗
You need not state the reason why you left your former companies.	✗	
Is this sentence is ok?: 'My responsibilities included training staff in new customer-care procedures.'		✗
Is this sentence is ok?: 'Successfully trained staff in new customer-care procedures.'	✗	

TASK 4: The open testimonial and how to read it

1. Mr B. has always managed well with his superiors.
   B. He adapts to his superior at any price.
2. He always deals with his work in a right and proper way.
   A. He does not have any initiative, he is a typical bureaucrat.
3. Mr B. is a sociable colleague.
   B. He prefers talking and drinking to work.
4. He has a sense of what is essential.
   A. He has a strongly developed sense of target-orientation.
5. He is diligent and knows how to sell himself.
   A. He blows up his importance.
6. He always tries to do his best to complete his tasks.
   A. He does his best but his best is never good enough.
7. He has the ability to motivate colleagues in a target-oriented way.
   B. He is a good leader of people.
8. He always fulfilled our expectations.
   B. He worked regularly and in a successful way.

TASK 5: Can you create the right atmosphere?

Greetings

Guten Tag. Mein Name ist Bright.	How *do you do*? My name's Bright.
Freut mich, Sie kennen zu lernen, Herr Bright.	Pleased to *meet* you, Mr Bright.
Ganz meinerseits.	The pleasure *is mine*.

Icebreakers

Haben Sie unsere Firma gleich gefunden?	*Did you* find our company straight away?
Dank Ihrer genauen Beschreibung hatte ich keine Probleme.	I *didn't have* any trouble thanks to your clear instructions.
Nehmen Sie doch bitte Platz.	Please *have a seat*.
Darf ich Ihnen etwas zum Trinken anbieten? Kaffee, Tee oder sonst etwas?	*May* I *offer* you something to drink? Coffee, tea or something else?

Ich nehme das Gleiche wie Sie. Ich schlage vor, wir lassen die Förmlichkeiten beiseite.	*I'll have* the same as you. I *suggest* we drop the formalities.

TASK 6: Beef up your word power

1. You interview candidates, applicants or *interviewees.*
2. If they are good you hire, employ or *recruit* them.
3. The verb is *to take*: You can *take* notes, time, decisions and risks.
4. If a candidate *embellishes* the facts he is not honest.
5. Expanding notes means **B.** completing them
6. Enlarging facts in one's CV means **C.** commenting on the facts.

MODULE 7

TASK 1: Business phrases to remember

Neuerungen einführen	*introduce* innovations
eine neue Drehtür planen	*design* a new revolving door
die Markteinführung sollte in einer Woche sein	the *launch* was to be in a week's time
ein wichtiger Querschnitt unserer Kundschaft	an important *cross-section* of our customers
jemandem die Drehtür in Aktion zeigen	show someone the revolver *in action*.
den Tagungsort inspizieren	to inspect the *venue*

TASK 2: What went wrong?

1. It was in Ramsch's apartment where the fate of the presentation was sealed. With his decision to do it spontaneously, to "risk" it, he set all the following problems into motion. Even though it takes more time it is necessary to prepare and write up the presentation. The facts must be organised in logical sequence, language must be clear and simple. The key points must be emphasised in some way.
2. Here Ramsch, perhaps because he is not properly prepared, is nervous. He tries to make a joke, first with a word-play (present, past, future) and then with the quotation from the beer advert. It doesn't work and the listeners are frustrated. By the way, Ramsch should have thought more about his audience. Key-accounts, buyers short of time etc. Having written out the presentation, Ramsch should have practised it a couple of times (perhaps with a tape recording).
3. The problem here is that Ramsch did not choose his aids carefully. Again this leads back to his bad decision in the preparation phase. Flipcharts can be used in presentations. It gives spontaneous information, but not for whole diagrams and designs. If used for detail, the flipchart should be prepared in advance. Therefore, Ramsch should have used the OHP or even a video, if one was available. At this stage of the presentation while writing on the flipchart he was standing between the audience and the flipchart, a classical presentation error. And last but not least his writing was too small or too untidy. He did not communicate effectively.
4. Issue number four is concerned with timing. He had talked too much, wasted time and was therefore forced to hurry. Again his preparation is to blame. The answer: practise the presentation with a watch to get the timing right.
5. Ramsch came into the conference in a hurry so he hadn't had time to inspect his venue. It's vital to know your venue. This includes locating power points, lowering blinds for OHPs, videos, checking whether the flipchart, OHP can be seen by all, a table for handouts, checking the acoustics. And one point in this case was to inspect the door system just in case something is defective.

TASK 3: Introduce yourself

My name is David Ramsch.
I *have been* in the revolving door business *for* three years.
I *know* your problems *since* I was a sales manager *like* most of you.
I'm *no more* expert in this field *than* you are.

TASK 4: Welcome the audience

On behalf of our company I'd like to welcome you all here to our demonstration.
We're very *happy* to have you *with* us today.
I'm so glad that we have the *opportunity* to *discuss* this matter.
I *appreciate* that you're sacrificing one hour of your *valuable* time to listen to me.

TASK 5: Announce the purpose of the presentation

The *topic / subject* of this presentation is the breakthrough *in the field* of sliding doors.
I'm trying to give you an *overview of* our company's services.
In my presentation I'*ll be trying* to explain a new way of installing doors.
Don't *hesitate* to *interrupt* me when you have a question.

TASK 6: Explain the structure

My presentation will be in three *main parts.*
I'll be *developing* the three *stages* of our SX1.
To *begin with*, let me show you the control panel.
Firstly, I'd like to ... Secondly, we can ... And I'll *finish* with ...

TASK 7: Conclusion

I'd like to round off *by saying* ...
Let me end by saying that ...
I'd like to *conclude* by *stating* that ...
So that was it *for today*. Thank you for your *attention*, Ladies and Gentlemen.

MODULE 8

TASK 1: Telephone phrases to remember

Was kann ich für Sie tun?	*Can* I *help* you?
Ich rufe im Auftrag von Herrn X an.	I'm ringing *on behalf* of Mr X.
Verbinden Sie mich bitte mit Herrn Y.	Please *put* me *through* to Mr Y.
Er ist leider nicht an seinem Platz.	I'm afraid he's not *at* his *desk*.
Könnten Sie Herrn Y etwas ausrichten?	Could you *take* a message for Mr Y?
Oh, man hat mich aus der Leitung geschmissen / getrennt.	Oh, they've *cut* me *off*.

TASK 2: Would you have got it right?

This is all about communicating clearly over the phone for the first time.

1. It's only good manners to apologise for keeping the caller waiting. The operator should not carry on as if it is all perfectly normal. The apology will make the customer feel respected. "Sir, I'm sorry to keep you waiting. I was talking to ..."
2. She should have said, for example, "Good morning, this is Busoom Ltd. How can I help you? (How can I be of help / Who would you like to speak to?)"
3. The problem with Cocky's call is that she did not prepare it. When you phone somebody on business you should write out your points. Make sure you have all the information you might need to answer any questions. Check that it is the right time to phone. Cocky's phone call should have gone something like this:

   C: Hello, my name is Ellen Cocky from Combinations. Last week I sent you information on our special English language coaching seminars. I think you know our seminar trainer Dr Bossybitch.

   H: Yes, thank you. I believe we have received the information. Actually I am not the right man. I'll put you through to ...

4. It's not good to drop names. The recipient of the advertising information may remember the offer, but he's unlikely to keep a name in mind. It's not an important piece of information. Don't waste the time of your potential customer!
5. Cocky should have done some research to find out who the relevant partner is, for example by asking the company's receptionist.

TASK 3: Telephoning effectively

1. Answering the phone

Guten Tag. Was kann ich für Sie tun?	Hello. How *can I help* you?

2. Tell them who you are

Spreche ich mit Herrn X?	Hello? *Is that* Mr X?

3. Identifying the caller

Darf ich um Ihren Namen bitten?	May I *ask* who is calling?
Entschuldigen Sie, ich habe Ihren Namen nicht richtig verstanden.	I'm sorry, sir. I didn't quite *catch* your name.

4. Who do you want to speak to?

Geben Sie mir bitte Ihre Verkaufsabteilung.	Could you *put* me *through* to your sales department, please?

5. Asking what it's about

Darf ich nach dem Grund Ihres Anrufs fragen?	May I ask the *purpose* of *your* call?

6. Getting through the waiting periods

Frau Potter spricht gerade auf einer anderen Leitung.	Mrs Potter is *speaking* on *another line.*
Tut mir sehr Leid, aber es wird gerade gesprochen.	I'm awfully sorry, but the line is *busy / engaged.*

7. Leaving a message

Würden Sie ihm bitte ausrichten, dass Bob Marley angerufen hat?	Would you please *tell* him that Bob Marley *called*?

8. Wrong number

Entschuldigen Sie bitte, ich muss mich wohl verwählt haben.	I beg your pardon, I must have *dialled* the wrong number.

9. Communication problems

Könnten Sie bitte langsamer sprechen?	Could you speak *more slowly*, please?
Meinen Sie November oder September?	Do you *mean* November or September?
Könnten Sie das buchstabieren?	Could you *spell* that out for me?

TASK 4: Let's get it right

1. May I assist you somehow other?

TASK 5: Typical German!

1. What can *I do for you*? (word order!)
2. Who *would you like to speak to*?
3. I'd like to speak to your boss, ~~if it goes~~ if possible.
4. I'm sorry, sir. I ~~haven't~~ quite ~~caught~~ your name.
   I *didn't* quite *catch* your name. (past tense)
5. ~~Do I speak~~ to Doors Inc.?
   Am I speaking to Doors Inc.? (aspect; present progressive, weil gerade, im Augenblick)
6. ~~Are you spelling~~ Brian with an 'i' or a 'y'?
   Do you spell Brian with an 'i' or a 'y'? (aspect; simple present, da immer so)

MODULE 9

TASK 1: Business phrases to remember

den Betrieb aufhalten	block *up* work-*processes*
Da liegt ein Missverständnis vor.	There's some misunderstanding *going on.*
Da ist ein Körnchen Wahrheit dran.	There's a *grain* of *truth* in it.
jemandem etwas ausrichten	*take* a message *for* someone
Die Botschaft wurde gut aufgenommen.	The message went *down well.*
Anforderungen stellen	*set* standards
zusammengestaucht werden	be *on* the *carpet*

TASK 2: Getting the message

1. He is most sensitive that messages are not passed on accurately and in good time, and as a result the company loses money and maybe customers.
2. He wants the staff to use standardised forms for e-mails and memos, reports etc. where all the data is entered in the same places.
3. **A.** I was totally shocked, anything, even a light-weight thing would have pushed me over.
   B. "It will go down" means "it will be accepted". "They will go down" means the employees will sink, perhaps be fired.

TASK 3: What do you know about internal memoranda?

Take a stand

	Yes	No
1. Should you prepare a memorandum at the end of conversations etc? (Notes in handwriting are sufficient in most cases.)		✗
2. Mr Rum messed up a presentation. Do you write him a memo? (Don't criticise on the phone or in writing!)		✗
3. Do you keep the list of recipients as short as possible. (Of course)	✗	

4. If you want to keep a memo secret do you mark it "To whom it may concern"?		✗
5. If the memo is top secret, do you mark it "Confidential". (If you want it widely read, do it. Put the copies into envelopes and mark them "Addressee to open".)		✗
6. Memos should only be read in the office. Memos may be taken home and on trips. (You can read them on the train, taxi or plane.)		✗
7. Is this sentence memo style? *Consideration should be given to the possibility of carrying into effect plan B as suggested by the consultants.* (Shorter, therefore better: *Should we carry out plan B as suggested by consultants?*)		✗
8. If your memo is more than two pages do you add a contents list?	✗	
9. Should you leave generous space between paragraphs and at the bottom of the page? (Allow reader to make notes.)	✗	
10. Do you leave a wide margin on both sides of the page? (Allow reader to make notes.)	✗	

TASK 4: The perfect memo

1. They *violate* a cardinal rule of business etiquette:
2. Don't *waste* your colleagues' time!
3. Think *twice* before you write a memorandum.
4. If you need *immediate* feedback, make a telephone call or ...
5. ... arrange an *appointment*.
6. Write a memo only if you need the memo as *proof* that you have taken action.
7. ... if you want to express or *emphasize* your views.
8. ... if you want to put forward *suggestions*.
9. ... if you want to *supply* information that would otherwise take too long to reach all who need it.

TASK 5: The structure of the memo

1. State the *purpose.*
2. *Subject*: Improving product presentations
3. The list of *addressees*,
4. the copy list, should be *limited* to those who need the information.
5. *Contents*
6. If your memo has more than two pages, give the reader an *overview.*
7. How to *remedy* shortcomings
8. *Heading*
9. Leave wide *margins* on both sides of the page.

TASK 6: How would Churchill have said it

1. We should bear in mind / we should not forget / we should remember.
2. Should we carry out plan B?

MODULE 10

TASK 1: Did you get the message?

1. Loud has obviously had problems with some of his colleagues. Perhaps he has been shouting at people. "They don't understand his problems." He's defensive from the outset. Seaweed's best reaction should be to calm him, to make clear that nobody has "denounced" him. Read on to find out how Seaweed reacted.
2. By using this phrase and describing Loud's possible reaction Seaweed creates an atmosphere of understanding and trust. He does not create a climate of accusation, which is so destructive for real communication.
3. The employee thinks he should have more money. Actually, we all think we should have more money. Seaweed's strategy is first to agree with Loud, then to offer a useful alternative that might actually solve the

problem. And the offer of the time planning seminar is done in such a way that it is not forced onto Loud. However, Seaweed should have prompted the solution, not suggested it.

4. Seaweed uses words like "let us" and "we" to show Loud that they are all involved, he is not alone with his trouble. "It's not just you suffering. Don't worry." Again he doesn't rush Loud. "If you agree, I'd suggest ..." He's not accusing but rather suggesting a solution that everybody is involved in.
5. "Great ..." The exclamation "great" shows motivation on the part of Seaweed. It helps Loud to feel "needed". Then Seaweed introduces the personal topic in an anonymous way. "I heard it on the grapevine." Seaweed hopes to relax Loud, and certainly not to give the impression that he is interfering. Seaweed would like to have Loud's confidence and uses this collective form: "... why don't we sit together with ...?"

TASK 2: Business phrases to remember

Spannungen mit Angestellten	*tension* with employees
persönlich einschreiten	*intervene* personally
Ziele stecken	*set* goals
Er schafft es nicht, es ist ihm nicht möglich.	He can't *manage*.
Berichte aus den Abteilungen	*reports* from the *departments*

TASK 3: Bits and pieces

etwas gerüchteweise hören	hear something *on* the grapevine
Tun Sie, was Sie für richtig halten.	Do *as* you see fit.
sich damit sofort befassen	deal *with* it *on* the spot
Tipps, wie man die Leistung verbessert	tips *on how* to improve performance

TASK 4: Phrases for counsellors – personal problems

1. How to start the conversation

Es geht mich vielleicht nichts an, aber ...	Perhaps it's not my *business*, but ...
Ich sollte mich vielleicht nicht einmischen, aber ...	Perhaps I should keep my *nose* out of it, but ...
Halten Sie mich bitte nicht für neugierig, aber ...	Don't think I'm sticking my *nose* in, but ...
Halten Sie mich bitte nicht für neugierig, aber ...	Don't think I'm being *nosy*, but ...

2. Expressing sympathy

Ich habe das Gefühl, Sie bedrückt etwas.	I think you've got something on your *mind*.
Sie sind mit Ihren Gedanken in der letzten Zeit ganz woanders.	In the last few days you've had your *mind* on something else.
Haben Sie Sorgen?	Are you *worried* about something?
Sie machen ein Gesicht wie drei Tage Regenwetter.	You're really going around with a long *face*.

3. Creating an atmosphere of confidence

Sie können ganz offen sprechen.	You can speak *openly / frankly*.
Wir sollten uns einmal unter vier Augen unterhalten.	We should talk about it *privately*.
Es bleibt alles unter uns.	We'll keep it to *ourselves*.
unter vier Augen	just *between* you and me
Wo drückt der Schuh?	What's *bothering* you?
Wir sind doch keine Unmenschen.	We aren't *monsters*, you know.

4. Offering a shoulder to cry on

Nehmen Sie mein Taschentuch.	Use my *handkerchief*.
Ich kann mir vorstellen, wie Ihnen zumute ist.	I can *imagine* how you feel.

Das kann jedem von uns passieren.	It can *happen* to anyone. These things can *happen*.
Nichts wird so heiß gegessen, wie es gekocht wird.	It's never *as* bad *as* it seems.
Lassen Sie sich ruhig Zeit.	*Take* your time.

5. Offering support

Kann ich irgendetwas für Sie tun?	Is there anything *at all* I can do?
Kann ich Ihnen irgendwie helfen?	Can I *be of* help somehow?
Gibt es etwas, das ich tun könnte?	Can I help in *any* way?

6. Looking for a solution

Es gibt immer einen Ausweg.	There's always some *way out*.
Wir werden gemeinsam eine Lösung finden.	We'll find a *solution* together.
Haben Sie schon einmal mit dem Betriebsrat gesprochen?	Have you already spoken to the *works council*?
Möchten Sie, dass ich mit … spreche?	Do you *want me* to speak to …?
Lassen Sie das unseren Justiziar machen, dazu ist er da.	Our *legal advisor* should do it. That's what he's paid for.
Nach Regen kommt Sonnenschein.	Every *cloud* has a silver lining.
Kommt Zeit, kommt Rat.	Time will *tell*.

TASK 5: How good a coach are you?

	Yes	No
1. You should meet staff regularly at least monthly.	✗	
2. These meetings should always be informal.		✗
3. Coaching means annual appraisals and performance reviews.		✗
4. Give them the performance review a week beforehand.	✗	
5. Listen and avoid any confrontation.		✗
6. The main aim of coaching is to improve the working climate.		✗

7.	The main aim of coaching is to improve performance.		✗
8.	You shouldn't hesitate to discuss any weaknesses of an employee.	✗	
9.	Coaching should be formal. Prepare an agenda.	✗	
10.	Don't coach without the consent of the employee.	✗	

TASK 6: How good a counsellor are you?

	Take a stand	Yes	No
1.	Your secretary has a problem. You discuss it with her.	✗	
2.	If the problem affects her job you inform your boss.		✗
3.	You give her sound advice; you appeal to reason and logic.		✗
4.	If you want to influence her, appeal to emotions.	✗	
5.	It is your job to suggest a solution to her problem.		✗
6.	Counselling is help to help herself. Let her find a solution.	✗	
7.	Offer several ways to reach the goal. Leave her the choice.	✗	
8.	Help to establish a plan for reaching the goal.	✗	
9.	Observe over a period of time how she is coping.	✗	
10.	Set a deadline by which you expect her to have solved the problem.		✗

MODULE 11

TASK 1: How good is your memory?

Aufmerksamkeit der Öffentlichkeit erregen	*get* into the public eye
jemanden auf sich aufmerksam machen	*catch* someone's attention
Ergebnisse beobachten / verfolgen	*monitor* results
zurück zu unserem Thema	*back* to our topic
den Absatz fördern	*support* sales

TASK 2: Presenting the company

1. We are a *medium-sized* company.
2. Our company *was founded* 25 years ago.
3. Our company *has expanded* rapidly.
4. We have *subsidiaries* located in five cities.
5. The company *employs* over two hundred people.
6. We supply models through *retail outlets* all over Britain.
7. Our principal *operations* are in revolving and sliding doors.
8. We pride ourselves in being the *market leader.*

TASK 3: First steps towards a mission statement

1. suppliers
2. (it) employs
3. subsidiaries
4. foundation
5. has grown
6. demands
7. requirements
8. needs
9. (has) diversified
10. (has) innovated
11. range
12. breakthrough
13. attention
14. users
15. convey

TASK 4: Communication quiz

1. trade shows, trade fairs
2. sponsoring, sponsorship
3. Public Relations
4. leafleting
5. direct mailing
6. face-to-face contact
7. It's a fact: The most effective advertising is positive word-of-mouth.
8. False: Press releases are much cheaper than advertising in the media.
9. False: The quality of press releases decides whether it will be published or not.

MODULE 12

TASK 1: Sit back and think

1. He tries to make a different opening, not just to open with his typical annual, automatic "thank-you" to the staff. He makes it clear that this time there are also more serious matters to deal with.
2. His main theme is the question of work in our lives and what it can mean for us. However, Hardman wants to use this general theme as a springboard for deeper issues.
3. Hardman's real goal in talking about work is to make his staff aware that it is not work or putting in hours that is important, but rather the quality and effectiveness of that work.
4. It is spoken communication. Therefore Hardman uses short forms, "it is" becomes "it's", "we have" becomes "we've" etc. He also uses words which fit more into spoken language, for example, "wherewithal" instead of "financial means".
   Hardman also uses repetition, that is he uses two or three different words to express one idea: money = *salary, wages, income, whatever you prefer to call it.*
5. He refers to the company as a boat. "He or she doesn't actually row the boat forward. They hold it back." This brings alive the idea of cooperation and one entity.
   The other image is of the "industrial civil servant", a lazy or at least unmotivated clerk doing a minimum of work in some "Amt" somewhere.

TASK 2: Business phrases to remember

Währungskurse	*currency* rates
Kunden verlieren	*lose* customers
Zeit investieren	*put* in time
Wir können das nicht beeinflussen.	We can't *impact* on that.
den Termin für eine Besprechung festsetzen	*fix* a *date* for a meeting

seine Lohntüte bekommen	*get* one's *wage package*
Das Produktionszentrum fasst 150 Menschen.	The production centre *accommodates* 150 people.
Werbefeldzug der Konkurrenten	sales *drive* by *competitors*

TASK 3: Beef up your word power: opposites

there were ups	and *downs*
we lose customers	we *gain* / *win* customers
we are doing well	we are doing *badly*
a delivery is one day late	a delivery is one day *early*
hush a scandal up	bring it to the *light* of *day*

TASK 4: Streamlining the English

I think everybody knows	*as you all* know
the consequence is	the *bottom* line is
it is self-evident	it *goes* without *saying*
just wait and see	things will *take care of* themselves
I'll give you the exact figures later	I'll come to the figures *in some more detail* later

MODULE 13

TASK 1: Did you get the message?

1. We see early on in the dialogue that Seaweed has sent out invitations, minutes of the last meeting, and the agenda, and expects the participants to prepare, i.e., clear lines.
2. He gives clear instructions as to who should speak and what is expected. He organises well.
3. We can see this where the two department leaders are arguing about numbers and Seaweed intervenes to bring them back to reality. This way he defuses the situation indicates that he is a competent chairman.
4. He uses the typical phrase: "First I'd like to make a brief summary." Later he also adds "Let's now draw the meeting to a close".

TASK 2: Some steps in meetings

eine Einladung erhalten	*receive* / *get* an invitation
um Ruhe bitten	*call* to order
die Besprechung eröffnen	*open* the meeting
das Protokoll führen	*take* the *minutes*
eine Besprechung wieder in geordnete Bahnen lenken	*bring* a meeting to *order*
der erste Tagesordnungspunkt	the first *item* on the *agenda*
eine Besprechung schließen	*draw* the meeting to a *close*

TASK 3: In other words

head of selling	head of *sales*
customer service	*after-sales*
participant at a meeting	*attendee*
be in the chair	*chair* a meeting / *preside* over the meeting

TASK 4: How good is your memory?

1. May I *apologise* for the fact that Director X is *held up* by urgent business?
2. I'd like to *suggest / propose* that we add the following *items* to the *agenda*.
3. Could we *delete* item 3?
4. Can we *take* the *minutes as read*?
5. *As* you can see from the agenda there are three *decisions* to be *taken* today.

TASK 5: Do you remember these?

1. And where exactly do you *stand on* this *issue*, Bob?
2. Could we *adjourn* the meeting *to* Monday?
3. Perhaps we can discuss that at a *later date*.
4. I think our accountant would like to *make* a *point*.

TASK 6: What about these?

1. Those in favour *raise* their hands.
2. Any *abstentions*?
3. The motion is *rejected* by eight *votes* to three.
4. I *declare* the meeting *closed*.

TASK 7: Beef up your word power

invite to a meeting	*call* a meeting
discuss all the topics	*cover* all the topics
suggest a strategy	*propose* a strategy
adjourn a meeting	*postpone* a meeting
cancel an item on the agenda	*delete* an item

MODULE 14

TASK 1: Reading between the lines

1. Velvet is building bridges. She is linking to something in her partner's past which she has in common with her. In this case they are both acquainted with the same thing. This creates a feeling of security for both of them. In a second example they both have squash in common.
2. Friendly is using the "small-talk fade in" where she brings the conversation back to common experiences to reach safe ground again.
3. Velvet's words here are consciously or unconsciously working at getting information out of Friendly. She states what Hardman's worries are to get some sort of reaction from her partner. It's not meant in a bad way; it's a sort of information-collecting skill – and in this way Friendly becomes a "mouth". There are "mouths" and "moles" in small-talking and networking. A mole feeds info back to the management. A mouth passes info on from a source. In this case the source is the staff in general.
4. Friendly obviously does not want to talk about staff members. She uses the small-talk technique of exchanging old memories which the two speakers might have in common. It brings the two together and creates a link.

TASK 2: Get your verb forms right

Die unterstrichenen Ausdrücke sind Auslöser für die Verbformen.

1. I *have been working* at Busoom's for almost six weeks.
2. At the moment I'*m working* close to Hardman.
3. I'*m looking* for connections with worthwhile Busoomers. (at the moment)
4. I *went* to polytech in Wapperdale.
5. I'*ve been playing* squash for six years.
6. I *play* as often as I can.

TASK 3: Streamline your English

Do it if you want to be successful	This is the *key* to success.
The world is a village.	It's a *small* world, *isn't it*?
He got rid of his aggressions.	He *let* off *steam*.
He's a rough diamond but he's good at heart.	His *bark* is worse than his *bite*.
The new rule wasn't taken well.	It *went down* badly.

TASK 4: Let's take the first steps

You ask	He / she answers
Where is the conference room, please?	It's on the second floor.
Is that chair taken?	No, it isn't. Have a seat.
Do you know who the guest speaker is?	Sorry, I don't know him either.
How long will you be staying?	For two days.

TASK 5: Let's break the ice

Ask your question	He / she answers
Did you *have a good flight*?	No, it was rather bumpy.
May I *offer you something to drink*?	I'll have the same as you.
Would you *like to join us for* dinner this evening?	I'd love to, but I've got an another engagement.
How long *have you been in England*?	I've been in England for three days.

TASK 6: You are the host

Prosten Sie Ihrem Gast zu.	To *your good health! / Cheers!*
Sie glauben, dass er Computerexperte ist.	*You seem to be an expert on* computers.
Deuten Sie an, dass sich Ihre Geschäftsinteressen teilweise überlappen.	Obviously our *business interests overlap in some* areas.
Sagen Sie, dass eine Zusammenarbeit im beiderseitigen Interesse wäre.	I think *a cooperation is in my interest as well as yours.*

TASK 7: Small talk international

Nations	Mark
British, Americans	1
Chinese, Russians	3
French, Australians, Canadians	2
Finns, Swedes, Japanese	4
Mexicans, Peruvians, Argentinians	1
Germans	4

Source: Richard D. Lewis, *When Cultures collide*. London, 1996

MODULE 15

TASK 1: Reading between the lines

1. Ramsch realises that a negotiation must be practised, rehearsed, if possible in the form of the role-play. This creates confidence and a better understanding of the logic involved.
2. Ramsch knows he has to create a warm, responsive atmosphere where his partner feels relaxed. Negotiating often kills the appetite, but stimulates the thirst. So have drinks at hand.
3. Ramsch also builds bridges by talking about former successes that they have enjoyed together. He's creating a positive atmosphere.
4. The tactic is not to confront your "opponent", but rather to offer him an alliance in some way. Ramsch mentions that he has been thinking about Slippery's problems.("We've always found a way!")
5. Ramsch knows he will have problems with this topic (quality at Slippery's), so he tries to weaken his opponent's position by reporting a criticism of workmanship at Slippery's company.

TASK 2: Business phrases to remember

über die Preise diskutieren	*discuss* prices
vernünftige Preise erwarten	expect *reasonable* prices
die Mengen erhöhen	*increase* the quantities
von einem Problem Wind bekommen	*get* wind of the problem
beim Kunden zusammenbauen	*assemble* at the customer's site
Schadensersatz für verlorene Zeit leisten	*compensate* someone's lost time
fehlerhafte Teile umsonst ersetzen	*replace* defective parts *free* of *charge*

TASK 3: Beef up your word power

propose	make a *proposal*
supply spare parts	be a *supplier* of spare parts
specify the measurements and tolerances	the *specification* of measurements and tolerances
calculate the costs	hand in the *calculation* of the costs.
rehearse a presentation twice	make two *rehearsals*
know how to succeed	know the secret of *success*

TASK 4: Got a feeling for language?

1. Tom broke the window, but it was my *fault* for letting him play football in the house.
2. A hospital *blunder* led to 500 cancer patients getting the wrong radiation treatment.
3. The causes of many birth *defects* have not yet been discovered.
4. I think there are a few *errors / mistakes* in your calculations.
5. I accepted my father's *faults* because I loved him.
6. The letter had quite a few *mistakes / errors* in it.

The Oxford Advanced Learner's dictionary explains this as follows:
Mistake is the most general and used in most situations.
Error is used when talking about calculations, and in technical or formal contexts.
A *blunder* is a stupid or careless and quite serious mistake made because of bad judgement.
Fault emphasizes a person's responsibility for a mistake. A *fault* can also be an imperfection in a person or thing: There was a design fault in the train doors.
A *defect* is a serious imperfection.

TASK 5: What is the typical business verb?

1. *meet* a customer's requirements
2. *cover* customer needs
3. be *rated* best by a consumer magazine
4. *do* business together

TASK 6: More business verbs to remember

1. *come* to an agreement
2. *strike* a compromise
3. *meet* someone halfway
4. *make* certain concessions
5. *accept* an offer
6. *agree* to a suggestion

MODULE 16

TASK 1: What's your comment?

1. The advert is woolly and does not bring over to the customer what Busoom wants to say.
2. He shortens sentences to catchy phrases which are well-known in the business e.g., leading edge.
3. The short, compact phrases lead towards the last two lines. The second line to last, a sort of climax, states the product names. The final line attracts the attention of the potential buyer to vital features of the products and company.

TASK 2: Business phrases to remember

eine Agentur beauftragen	*commission* an agency
die neueste Technologie integrieren	integrate the *latest* technology
in der Technologie führend sein	be a *leader* in technology

Wir sind anspruchsvoller.	We're more *upmarket.*
die Zielgruppe ausmachen	identify the *target* group
potenzielle Kunden erreichen	*get across* to potential customers
einen großen technologischen Vorsprung haben	have a leading *edge* technology

TASK 3: Increase your word power

noun	verb
advertisement	advertise
success	succeed
purchase	purchase
decision	decide

TASK 4: Idiomatic English

kurz gesagt, in einem Wort	to put it in a *nutshell*
jemandem einen Hinweis geben	give someone a *pointer*
etwas den letzten Schliff geben	tidy up the *edges*

TASK 5: Preparing our psychologist's corner

1. appeal — **B.** be attractive or interesting to someone
2. benefits — **A.** be of advantage or use to someone
3. target — **D.** aim at the prospective customer
4. trigger — **E.** be the cause of / start something
5. convey — **C.** transmit an idea

MODULE 17

TASK 1: Business phrases to remember

zur Sache kommen	come to the *point*
die Ergebnisse der Forschung	the results of the *research*
die Ergebnisse einer Umfrage	the findings of a *survey*
eine Produktionsstätte einrichten	*set up* a small production unit
die Arbeitslosigkeit verringern	*reduce* unemployment
die Kosten niedrig halten	*keep* costs *down*
Wir wollen keine Fixkosten.	We don't want *overheads / fixed costs.*
Fortschritte machen	make *progress*

TASK 2: What do they understand by truth?

	Nation		Attitude towards truth
1	Italy, France	D	smooth social relationship are more important than the truth
2	Britain	C	the truth is the truth as long it doesn't rock the boat (create unnecessary problems)
3	Japan	B	adherence to the truth must not destroy the harmony and balance of society
4	China	A	there is no absolute truth

TASK 3: Understanding the Americans

	American English		British English
1.	You're the CEO.	G	You are the managing director.
2.	Sure!	H	Of course!
3.	How does that grab you?	B	What do you think of that?
4.	Bean-counters drive me mad.	A	Accountants can be frustrating.
5.	You're talking bullshit.	C	I'm not quite with you on that.

6.	Jack'll blow his top.	I	Our chairman might disagree.
7.	You gotta be kidding!	E	How interesting, however ...
8.	Got some goodies for you.	F	We've some fine products to offer to you.
9.	I tell you, I can walk away from this deal.	D	I'm afraid, we all have to do our homework first.

TASK 4: Cultural awareness test

Meetings the American way – Meetings the German way **A or G?**

1.	They start with humour, jokes, wisecracks.	A
2.	They start with introductions and the agenda; no jokes.	G
3.	They expect to be addressed with their titles.	G
4.	Their meetings have a beginning, a middle and an end; one thing at a time, step by step.	G
5.	They are quickly on first-name terms at the first meeting.	A
6.	They want you to put your cards on the table at once; no beating around the bush.	A
7.	Communication is explaining, asking questions, exchanging and testing views.	G
8.	Communication is a fight: they confront, provoke, they use sarcasm and kidding.	A
9.	They listen to an argument and reply with a counter-argument.	G
10.	They make an offer and expect a counter-offer.	A
11.	They want 'Yes' in principle; details can be settled later.	A
12.	They want to settle the details first and then take a decision.	G
13.	Everybody should come well-prepared. No surprises, no spontaneous presentations.	G
14.	They tend to start with presentations that listeners are not always prepared for.	A
15.	They expect clarity, reliability. They need time to deliberate and test the offers.	G
16.	They seek the instant deal; they wish to do the business as soon as possible.	A

TASK 5: How good a guest would you be?

Are these statements true (T) or false (F)? **T / F**

1.	If you are invited to an American home, you should bring flowers for the hostess. *Don't! It's a European custom. Ring them up and ask if you should bring a salad or dessert. If not, bring a box of chocolates or a souvenir from your country.*	**F**
2.	Americans normally wish each other "Good appetite" before they begin a meal together. *No, they don't. They might offer you the bowls and say "Help yourself". Some families hold hands and say a short prayer.*	**F**
3.	It is considered polite to leave a little bit of food on your plate when you have finished eating. *Don't! Your host might think you don't like the dish and be disappointed. However, in restaurants it is perfectly acceptable to leave food on your plate or even to ask for a doggy box to take home what you can't finish.*	**F**
4.	Guests usually offer to help in the kitchen. *Right! It is polite to ask if there is anything you can help with around the house.*	**T**
5.	You need to go to the toilet? Don't ask, *"May I use your toilet, please?"* The word toilet sounds unpleasant to American ears. In private homes you ask *"May I use your bathroom?"* In restaurants it is the restroom, the men's room or the ladies' room.	**F**
6.	When they ask you "How do you like the USA?" they expect you to give a frank and honest answer. *No, they don't, so don't mention the negative sides of the country. They expect you to give a short positive answer. This doesn't only apply to the US. If a family is kind enough to invite you, they don't want to hear negative things from the foreign guest.*	**F**
7.	If you feel hot, you may ask if you can open a door or a window, although almost all rooms are air-conditioned.	**T**

Yes, you may. In American offices, schools and private homes doors are usually left open. A closed door is the sign that a room is occupied. So leave the door of the bathroom (toilet) open if you aren't using it. Other members of the family might be waiting impatiently for someone to come out.

TASK 6: Would you know what you get to eat there?

	American English		British English
1	French fries	E	chips
2	cookie	C	biscuit
3	biscuit	D	scone
4	surf-and-turf	A	steak and lobster
5	potato chips	B	crisps

MODULE 18

Hardman's quiz

1. A. is the polite way to start, but use B. if it does'nt work. C. is bad-mannered.
2. B. will save the time and trouble of calling a meeting again, if your colleague still objects, go to C.
3. C. is by far the most diplomatic and practical strategy. If necessary, pretend to have stomach pains – but not as a result of too much alcohol.
4. A. is the best unless you fear that the business might be compromised in some way in which case you should adopt B.
5. C. is a polite and thoughtful strategy as long as your contact keeps it confidential.
6. C. should give both parties an opportunity to put things right without it necessarily being the prime purpose of the call.

7. B. is best since you should always adopt a "business as usual" strategy until the other person decides to share a confidence with you.
8. C. because it's better to be discreet.
9. B. should be possible if you are careful. You shouldn't directly contradict him, but offer an alternative point of view.
10. B. is the most practical, but perhaps you should be looking around in the company for a job which suits you better.